The Wolfhound Book of Irish Poems for Young People

Selected by
Bridie Quinn & Seamus Cashman

WOLFHOUND PRESS

Reprinted 1992
This edition 1987, 1990
Paperback edition 1982
© 1975 Wolfhound Press
All editorial matter © 1975 Bridie Quinn and Seamus Cashman
Illustrations © 1975 Wolfhound Press
All rights reserved.
ISBN 0 86327 002 6

Printed in Ireland by Colour Books Ltd.

CONTENTS

List of Poems and Poets   6
Subject Index   10
A Word in Your Ear!   13
Poems   17
Notes and Explanations   175
Biographies   178
Editors' Note and Acknowledgments   184
First-line Index   186
Title Index   191

No separate index of poets is provided since poems
are arranged alphabetically by poet. Entries for
individual poets are readily located by reference
to the 'List of poems and poets'.

LIST OF POEMS AND POETS

The Mystery	Douglas Hyde	1
Pangur Bán	Robin Flower	2
The Hermit's Song	Frank O'Connor	3
My Story	Brendan Kennelly	4
God's Praises		5
The Blackbird by Belfast Lough	Frank O'Connor	6
The Fairies in New Ross	Anonymous	7
The Bubble	William Allingham	8
The Fairies		9
Four Ducks on a Pond		10
My Ship	Christy Brown	11
The Animals	George Buchanan	12
I wish and I wish	Joseph Campbell	13
Three Colts Exercising		14
The Blind Man at the Fair		15
Butterfly in the Fields		16
The Planter's Daughter	Austin Clarke	17
The Last Irish Snake		18
Black Tassels	Padraic Colum	19
The Old Woman of the Roads		20
The Terrible Robber Men		21
A Drover		22
Evidence	Eiléan Ní Chuilleanáin	23
Chorus of Spirits	George Darley	24
Lament for the Death of Eoghan Ruadh O'Neill	Thomas Davis	25
A Ballad of Athlone	Aubrey De Vere	26
The March to Kinsale		27
Boy Bathing	Denis Devlin	28
The Scarecrow	H. L. Doak	29
Still Life with Ashtray	Des Egan	30
The Fly in the Tower		31

The Pets	Robert Farren	32
Lament for the Death of Thomas Davis	Samuel Ferguson	33
The Crab Tree	Oliver Gogarty	34
Golden Stockings		35
Galway		36
The Village Schoolmaster	Oliver Goldsmith	37
The Little Waves of Breffny	Eva Gore-Booth	38
Herring is King	A. P. Graves	39
Prayer at Morning	Michael Hartnett	40
The Night before Patricia's Funeral		41
Requiem for the Croppies	Seamus Heaney	42
The Diviner		43
Thatcher		44
The Forge		45
Whinlands		46
Load	John Hewitt	47
Grace before Beer	F.R. Higgins	48
Dotage		49
Above		50
The Old Jockey		51
The Sunflower	Nora Hopper	52
The Toy Horse	Valentin Iremonger	53
Saint Fiacre	John Irvine	54
A Rathlin Cradle Song		55
Goldenhair	James Joyce	56
The Noise of Waters		57
Patrick Maguire	Patrick Kavanagh	58
My Room		59
Beech Tree		60
Autumn's End	John B. Keane	61
Caoch the Piper	John Keegan	62

Getting Up Early	Brendan Kennelly	63
Sea		64
Girl in a Rope		65
Poem from a Three-Year Old		66
Lightning		67
Leaf-Eater	Thomas Kinsella	68
Combat of Ferdia and Cúchulainn		69
Dick King		70
Tara		71
An Exile's Mother	Emily Lawless	72
A Dream Dance	Francis Ledwidge	73
At Currabwee		74
Boys	Winifred M. Letts	75
A Soft Day		76
Spring, the Travelling Man		77
Badger	Michael Longley	78
A Poaching Song	Donagh MacDonagh	79
John-John	Thomas MacDonagh	80
The Country Funeral	M.J. MacManus	81
County Sligo	Louis MacNiece	82
Glass Falling		83
Prognosis		84
A Dying Art	Derek Mahon	85
Roisin Dubh	James Clarence Mangan	86
O'Tuomy's Drinking Song		87
The Woman of Three Cows		88
Mountain Shapes	Alice Milligan	89
Sea Changes	John Montague	90
Time Out		91
What a View		92
A Canadian Boat Song	Thomas Moore	93
Let Erin Remember		94
Years Later	Richard Murphy	95
High Island		96
Kilcash	Frank O'Connor	97

The Water-Vole	D. J. O'Sullivan	98
Winter in Dublin		99
Soliloquy of a Lighthouse — Keeper		100
Mosaic		101
Money Spiders		102
Silhouettes		103
The Lamplighter	Seumas O'Sullivan	104
A Piper		105
The Sheep		106
Tortoise	Basil Payne	107
Dead Cat		108
Fun and Games		109
The Wayfarer	Padraic Pearse	110
Lullaby of a Woman of the Mountains		111
See the Crocus' Golden Cup	Joseph Mary Plunkett	112
I see His Blood upon the Rose		113
The Journey of the Magi	W. R. Rodgers	114
Now there stood by the Cross of Jesus his Mother		115
About the ninth hour ...		116
The Dead at Clonmacnois	T. W. Rolleston	117
Song of Maelduin		118
Frolic	George Russell(AE)	119
Joe's No Saint	John D. Sheridan	120
Smith's Song	George Sigerson	121
The Main-Deep	James Stephens	122
The Goat Paths		123
Etched in Frost		124
The Fifteen Acres		125
The Snare		126

Herrings	Jonathan Swift	127
A Riddle		128
Patch-Shaneen	J. M. Synge	129
Sheep and Lambs	Katherine Tynan	130
The Witch		131
The Children of Lir		132
Les Silhouettes	Oscar Wilde	133
The Painting		134
The Fiddler of Dooney	W. B. Yeats	135
The Cat and the Moon		136
To a Squirrel at Kyle-na-no		137
The Song of the Old Mother		138
The Song of Wandering Aengus		139

SUBJECT GUIDE

(This list is intended only as a general guide to assist readers to find poems dealing with particular subjects.)

ANIMALS/BIRDS
Above 50
Badger 78
Black Tassels 19
Leaf-Eater 68
Money Spiders 102
Sheep and Lambs 130
Silhouettes 103
The Animals 12
The Blackbird by Belfast
  Lough 6
The Cat and the Moon 136
The Fly in the Tower 31
The Goat Paths 123
The Sheep 106

The Snare 126
The Terrible Robber-men 21
The Water-Vole 98
Three Colts Exercising 14
Time Out 91
To a Squirrel at Kyle-na-no 137
Tortoise 107

BEAUTY
Getting up early 63
Goldenhair 56
The Painting 134
The Planter's Daughter 17
The Wayfarer 110

CHILDHOOD
Boys 75
Frolic 119
Fun and Games 109
Golden Stockings 35
Poem from a Three Year Old 66
The Toy Horse 53

DREAMS/FANTASY/
FOLKLORE/WISHES
A Dream Dance 73
Chorus of Spirits 24
At Currabwee 74
I Wish and I Wish 13
My Ship 11
The Fairies 9
The Fairies in New Ross 7
The Song of the Wandering
    Aengus 139

EVIDENCE
A Riddle 128
Evidence 23
Glass Falling 83
Still Life with Ashtray 30

GEOGRAPHICAL/PLACE
County Sligo 82
Dotage 49
Galway 36
High Island 96
Mountain Shapes 89
Tara 71
The Last Irish Snake 18
The Little Waves of Breffny 38
What a View 92
Winter in Dublin 99

HUMOUR
Grace Before Beer 48
O'Tuomy's Drinking Song 87
The Pets 32

LULLABY
A Rathlin Cradle Song 55
Lullaby of A Woman of the
    Mountains 111

MOVEMENT
Boy Bathing 28
Girl in a Rope 65
The Bubble 8
The Fifteen Acres 125
The Main-Deep 122
The Noise of Waters 57

MYSTERY
The Mystery 1

HISTORY/LEGEND
A Ballad of Athlone 26
An Exile's Mother 72
Combat of Ferdia and
    Cuchulainn 69
Kilcash 97
Lament for the Death of
    Eoghan Ruadh O'Neill 25
Lament for the Death of
    Thomas Davis 33
Let Erin Remember 94
Requiem for the Croppies 42
Roisin Dubh 86
The Children of Lir 132
The Dead of Clonmacnois 117
The March to Kinsale 27
The Song of Maelduin 118

NATURE

A Soft Day 76
Autumn's End 61
Beech Tree 60
Butterfly in the Fields 16
Etched in Frost 124
Four Ducks on a Pond 10
Les Silhouettes 133
Lightning 67
Load 47
Mosaic 101
My Story 4
Sea 64
Sea Changes 90
See the Crocus' Golden Cup 112
Spring, the Travelling Man 77
Saint Fiacre 54
The Crab Tree 33
The Hermit's Song 3
The Scarecrow 29
The Sunflower 52
Whinlands 46

PEOPLE/HOME/OCCUPATIONS

A Drover 22
A Dying Art 85
A Piper 105
A Poaching Song 79
A Canadian Boat Song 93
Caoch, The Piper 62
Dick King 70
Herring is King 39
Herrings 127
Joe's No Saint 120
John-John 80
My Room 59
Pangur Ban 2
Patch Shaneen 129

Patrick Maguire 58
Smith's Song 121
Soliloquy of a Lighthouse
   Keeper 100
Thatcher 44
The Blind Man at the Fair 15
The Country Funeral 81
The Diviner 43
The Fiddler of Dooney 135
The Forge 45
The Lamplighter 104
The Night Before Patricia's
   Funeral 41
The Old Jockey 51
The Old Woman of the Roads 20
The Song of the Old Mother 138
The Village Schoolmaster 37
The Woman of Three Cows 88
Years Later 95

PRAYER/RELIGIOUS

About the Ninth Hour ... 116
God's Praises 5
I See His Blood Upon the Rose 113
Now there Stood by the Cross
   of Jesus his Mother 115
Prayer at Morning 40
The Journey of the Magi 114

SUPERSTITION

Prognosis 84
The Witch 131

A WORD IN YOUR EAR!

All of the poems in this book were written by Irish
poets. Some of these poets lived hundreds of years ago;
some live and write in Ireland today. These writers
were monks, farmers, teachers, soldiers, housewives,
tradesmen, rich and poor, men and women who wrote
about their experiences, feelings and thoughts.

By reading what our poets have written, we can
experience what they experienced; we can discover
something new; we can see ordinary things in a new,
extraordinary way. What could be more ordinary than
to hear a blackbird singing, even in a city? Yet after
reading *The Blackbird by Belfast Lough*, written by an
unknown poet over eight hundred years ago, we
must wonder how something so commonplace can be
rendered so beautifully in words.

There are many poems here about ordinary
things — donkeys, crab trees, a blacksmith's forge, a
room, even about getting up early in the morning!
Other poems are about people, historical events,
legends, the seasons, places; and for humour and fun
read *O'Tuomy's Drinking Song, Boys, Fun and Games, Grace
before Beer* — and from Swift, the author of *Gulliver's
Travels,* there's a riddle which you must solve for your-
selves.

While poetry is something to enjoy simply by reading it quietly to ourselves, it can be enjoyed in other ways too. The best ways of all are to read the poem aloud, or to listen to it read aloud as you would listen to a song. Some poems can be 'acted' by two or more people, or even by groups of people together. These are the poems that tell a story — *Lament for the Death of Eoghan Ruadh O Neill, The Combat of Ferdia and Cuchulainn, Prognosis, The Ballad of Athlone* or *Patrick Maguire* — and poems that are full of movements (ideal for miming or speaking together in groups) like *Smith's Song, The Fifteen Acres, The Main-Deep, Above, The Bubble,* and others.

A few poems in this book will probably seem difficult to some readers at first. But don't be put off when you come across one that is hard, especially if you think it might be interesting. The thing to do is to read it a few times even if you don't fully understand it. Or better still, get a friend, brother, sister, parent or teacher to read it aloud to you. Listening to another person reading it will probably help you overcome difficult parts — as the old proverb goes, two heads are better than one. Remember that what you read in a short few minutes probably took the poet hours and hours to write! In any case if all the poems were simple and easy, this book would be no challlenge at all! In fact, in selecting the poems, we were not thinking of 'easy' and 'hard' ones, but of poems that we hope you will find both a challenge and a pleasure to read.

When you have read some of these poems, why
not write a poem yourself? There is much enjoyment
to be got from trying. Begin by choosing a subject.
You could pick one out of this book if you wish, but
it would be much better to choose as your subject
something about which you really want to write a
poem. Spend some time wondering what you might
say about the subject. While you're thinking and
wondering, words and phrases will begin to shape in
your mind. Write them down. At first, what you write
may not look like a poem; but with practice, poems will
will begin to take shape. And the poem you write will
say something that only you can say.

Now that you have read this far, it is time to
start browsing through the poems themselves. We
hope you enjoy each poem you read.

1 THE MYSTERY

I am the wind which breathes upon the sea,
I am the wave of the ocean,
I am the murmur of the billows,
I am the ox of the seven combats,
I am the vulture upon the rocks,
I am a beam of the sun,
I am the fairest of plants,
I am a wild boar in valour,
I am a salmon in the water,
I am a lake in the plain,
I am a word of science,
I am the point of the lance of battle,
I am the God who created in the head the fire.
Who is it who throws light into the meeting on the mountain?
Who announces the ages of the moon?
Who teaches the place where couches the sun?

(If not I)

Translated by Douglas Hyde

2 PANGUR BÁN

I and Pangur Bán, my cat,
'Tis a like task we are at;
Hunting mice is his delight,
Hunting words I sit all night.

Better far than praise of men
'Tis to sit with book and pen;
Pangur bears me no ill will,
He too plies his simple skill.

'Tis a merry thing to see
At our tasks how glad are we,
When at home we sit and find
Entertainment to our mind.

Oftentimes a mouse will stray
In the hero Pangur's way;
Oftentimes my keen thought set
Takes a meaning in its net.

'Gainst the wall he sets his eye
Full and fierce and sharp and sly;
'Gainst the wall of knowledge I
All my little wisdom try.

When a mouse darts from its den,
O how glad is Pangur then!
O what gladness do I prove
When I solve the doubts I love!

So in peace our tasks we ply,
Pangur Bán, my cat, and I;
In our arts we find our bliss,
I have mine and he has his.

Practice every day has made
Pangur perfect in his trade;
I get wisdom day and night
Turning darkness into light.

Translated by Robin Flower

3   THE HERMIT'S SONG

A hiding tuft, a green-barked yew-tree
      is my roof,
While nearby a great oak keeps me
      Tempest-proof.

I can pick my fruit from an apple
      Like an inn,
Or can fill my fist where hazels
      Shut me in.

A clear well beside me offers
      Best of drink,
And there grows a bed of cresses
      Near its brink.

Pigs and goats, the friendliest neighbours,
      Nestle near,
Wild swine come, or broods of badgers,
      Grazing deer.

All the gentry of the county
    Come to call!
And the foxes come behind them,
    Best of all.

To what meals the woods invite me
    All about!
There are water, herbs and cresses,
    Salmon, trout.

A clutch of eggs, sweet mast and honey
    Are my meat.
Heathberries and whortleberries
    For a sweet.

All that one could ask for comfort
    Round me grows,
There are hips and haws and strawberries,
    Nuts and sloes.

And when summer spreads its mantle
    What a sight!
Marjoram and leeks and pignuts,
    Juicy, bright.

Dainty redbreasts briskly forage
    Every bush,
Round and round my hut there flutter
    Swallow, thrush.

Bees and beetles, music-makers,
    Croon and strum;
Geese pass over, duck in autumn,
    Dark streams hum.

Angry wren, officious linnet
    And black-cap,
All industrious, and the woodpecker's
    Sturdy tap.

From the sea the gulls and herons
    Flutter in,
While in upland heather rises
    The grey hen.

In the year's most brilliant weather
    Heifers low
Through green fields, not driven nor beaten,
    Tranquil, slow.

In wreathed boughs the wind is whispering,
    Skies are blue,
Swans call, river water falling
    Is calling too.

Translated by Frank O'Connor

4   MY STORY

Here's my story; the stag cries,
Winter snarls as summer dies.

The wind bullies the low sun
In poor light; the seas moan.

Shapeless bracken is turning red,
The wildgoose raises its desperate head.

Birds' wings freeze where fields are hoary.
The world is ice. That's my story.

Translated by Brendan Kennelly

5   GOD'S PRAISES

Only a fool would fail
To praise God in His might
When the tiny mindless birds
Praise Him in their flight

Translated by Brendan Kennelly

6   THE BLACKBIRD BY BELFAST LOUGH

What little throat
Has framed that note?
What gold beak shot
    It far away?
A blackbird on
His leafy throne
Tossed it alone
    Across the bay.

Translated by Frank O'Connor

7 THE FAIRIES IN NEW ROSS
(County Wexford)

'When moonlight
Near midnight
Tips the rock and waving wood;
When moonlight
Near midnight
Silvers o'er the sleeping flood;
When yew-tops
With dew-drops
Sparkle o'er deserted graves;
'Tis then we fly
Through the welkin high,
Then we sail o'er the yellow waves.'

Anonymous

8 THE BUBBLE

See, the pretty Planet!
 Floating sphere!
Faintest breeze will fan it
 Far or near;

World as light as feather;
 Moonshine rays,
Rainbow tints together,
 As it plays;

Drooping, sinking, failing,
 Nigh to earth,
Mounting, whirling, sailing,
 Full of mirth;

Life there, welling, flowing,
 Waving round;
Pictures coming, going,
 Without sound.

Quick now, be this airy
 Globe repelled!
Never can the fairy
 Star be held.

Touched — it in a twinkle
 Disappears!
Leaving but a sprinkle,
 As of tears.

William Allingham

9 THE FAIRIES
(A Child's Song)

Up the airy mountain,
    Down the rushy glen,
We daren't go a-hunting
    For fear of little men;
Wee folk, good folk,
    Trooping all together;
Green jacket, red cap,
    And white owl's feather!

Down along the rocky shore
    Some make their home —
They live on crispy pancakes
    Of yellow tide-foam;
Some in the reeds
    Of the black mountain lake,
With frogs for their watch-dogs,
    All night awake.

High on the hill-top
    The old King sits;
He is now so old and gray
    He's nigh lost his wits.
With a bridge of white mist,
    Columbkill he crosses,
On his stately journeys
    From Slieveleague to Rosses;
Or going up with music
    On cold starry nights,
To sup with the Queen
    Of the gay Northern Lights.

By the craggy hill-side,
    Through the mosses bare,
They have planted thorn-trees
    For pleasure here and there.
Is any man so daring
    As dig one up in spite,
He shall find their sharpest thorns
    In his bed at night.

Up the airy mountain,
    Down the rushy glen,
We daren't go a-hunting
    For fear of little men;
Wee folk, good folk,
    Trooping all together;
Green jacket, red cap,
    And white owl's feather!

William Allingham

10   FOUR DUCKS ON A POND

Four ducks on a pond,
A grass-bank beyond,
A blue sky of spring,
White clouds on the wing:
What a little thing
To remember for years —
To remember with tears!

William Allingham

12   THE ANIMALS

The animals are herded slowly from green fields
to be eaten by gentlemen in restaurants. The fish
swim in the river for the pan of an experienced cook.
The wheat grows golden for loaves served at a fair price
in the shops. Even the birds in the trees
are aimed at by happy sportsmen. So the lovers of nature
make fatal advances towards the object of their affection.
And those living in cities who hate the country
and know where their bread-and-butter comes from don't care
as they walk in parks which are innocent of agriculture.

George Buchanan

11   MY SHIP

When I was a lad my bed was the ship
that voyaged me far through the star-dusted night
to lands forever beyond the world's lip
dark burning olive lands of delight
across blood-red oceans under the stars
lorded by the scarlet splendour of Mars.

It is only a bed now spread with eiderdown
and the sheets merciless chains holding me down.

Christy Brown

13   I WISH AND I WISH

I wish and I wish
And I wish I were
A honey bee
In the blue of the air,
Winging my way
At the mouth of the day
To the heather-marges
Of Loch-ciúin-bán;
Or a little green drake,
Or a silver swan,
Floating upon
The Stream of Aili,
And I to be swimming
Gaily, gaily.

Joseph Campbell

14 THREE COLTS EXERCISING IN A SIX-ACRE

Three colts exercising in a six-acre,
A hilly sweep of unfenced grass over the road.

What a picture they make against the skyline!
Necks stretched, hocks moving royally, tails flying;
Farm-lads up, and they crouching low on their withers.

I have a journey to go —
A lawyer to see, and a paper to sign in the Tontine —
But I slacken my pace to watch them.

Joseph Campbell

15   THE BLIND MAN AT THE FAIR

O to be blind!
To know the darkness that I know.
The stir I hear is empty wind,
The people idly come and go.

The sun is black, tho' warm and kind,
The horsemen ride, the streamers blow
Vainly in the fluky wind,
For all is darkness where I go.

The cattle bellow to their kind,
The mummers dance, the jugglers throw,
The thimble-rigger speaks his mind —
But all is darkness where I go.

I feel the touch of womankind,
Their dresses flow as white as snow;
But beauty is a withered rind,
For all is darkness where I go.

Last night the moon of Lammas shined,
Rising high and setting low;
But light is nothing to the blind —
All, all is darkness where they go.

White roads I walk with vacant mind,
White cloud-shapes round me drifting slow,
White lilies waving in the wind —
And darkness everywhere I go.

Joseph Campbell

Dallán Dé! Dallán Dé! —
Blind thing of God, why do you play?

Why do you flit about in the sun,
Darkling, painted, lovely one?

Whom do you know through shining hours?
What do you drink from secret flowers?

Are the unseen, seeing Others
Kinfolk, blessed fosterbrothers?

Whose is the burthen then you bear,
Filmy wing of the rayhot air?

Does the silk of your cast cocoon
Knit you to night more close than noon?

Fly you in tears, as Etáin flew,
Questing the king her girlhood knew?

Or drop in dream without hindsight,
Dead to the shadow, blind to light?

I am blind, and do not play —
Dallán Dé! Dallán Dé!

Joseph Campbell

17 THE PLANTER'S DAUGHTER

When night stirred the sea
And the fire brought a crowd in,
They say that her beauty
Was music in mouth
And few in the candlelight
Thought her too proud,
For the house of the planter
Is known by the trees.

Men that had seen her
Drank deep and were silent,
The women were speaking
Wherever she went —
As a bell that is rung
Or a wonder told shyly,
And O she was the Sunday
In every week.

Austin Clarke

18 THE LAST IRISH SNAKE

Far out to ocean Saint Patrick drove
The snakes from Ireland like a drove
Of shorthorns beyond the Great Blasket
Still clouding, unclouding, mountainous ridges.
He cursed them, tail and blastoderm
And with his crozier, rid
The rocky corners.   Coil over coil

Big and small families of outcasts,
Heads still held high, were hurrying,
No time to lay their eggs or cast
A skin, for his Latin lightened, hurled
More bolts at them: chariot wheels
Rolling downhill from the hub
By bush and boulder as they scattered
With green stripes, yellow dots of charlock,
Land-snakes, water-snakes all hubble-bubble,
Hundreds and hundreds of them scattered by
Jubilant hymn.
                But one old serpent
Sternly refused to be so servile
And leave Lough Allen, his habitat,
Although it flapped as the holy habit
Of the saint with rage. He showed his fang,
Indignant at these new-fangled ways,
And called to Aesculapius
In vain for he was quickly ousted.
Slowly he scaled and wriggled, eskered
Himself along alluvial soil,
Muddied, a trail of slime. Unsoiled
The water followed with bright reflection
Of intertwining blacks, of golden flecks.
People ten miles away at Roosky
Could hear him unearthing and their roosters
Clapped wings and dropped. The portly monster

Burrowing southward, left Lough Ree.
Wild duck came down, but saw no reeds.
He stopped to untangle at Portumna
And hold a public demonstration.
Scraw, scrub, thornbushes, thistles, briars
Rock, stone, were tossing up and down
As though he were Briarius
Twitched by a hundred dowsing rods,
His only form of rodomontade.
He worked like a huge excavator
With bucketed back digging a cavern
To hide in. Sacred skin was torn
To strips. The water, a brown-white torrent,
Was soon Lough Derg: another lake that
His blood was colouring with lake.
Onward, trundled the great Batrachian
By Foynes, Askeaton, Tarbet, Kilrush
Until the new River Shannon was rushing
South-westward, with small church, shanty,
And farm in flood. He passed Loop Head
And Kerry Head, loop after loop,
Then, left, between those far escarpments,
Day shining on an estuary,
And sank as if he were bedevilled,
Cabling along the ocean bed.

Austin Clarke

19 BLACK TASSELS

Black tassels, black tassels, upon the green tree,
The high tree, the ash-tree that tops the round hill,
Black tassels, blask tassels, and they are the crows.

Red streamers, red streamers along the hedgeways
Where roadways are claubered and stubbles are brown —
Red streamers, red streamers, and they are the haws.

A lone song, a high song that comes from the hedge,
That tries for a round and that falls on the turn —
A short song, the redbreast's, and Samhain's at hand.

Padraic Colum

20 THE OLD WOMAN OF THE ROADS

Oh, to have a little house!
To own the hearth and stool and all!
The heaped-up sods upon the fire,
The pile of turf against the wall!

To have a clock with weights and chains
And pendulum swinging up and down,
A dresser filled with shining delph,
Speckled and white and blue and brown!

I could be busy all the day
Clearing and sweeping the hearth and floor,
And fixing on their shelf again
My white and blue and speckled store!

I could be quiet there at night
Beside the fire and by myself,
Sure of a bed and loath to leave
The ticking clock and the shining delph!

Och! but I'm weary of mist and dark,
And roads where there's never a house nor bush,
And tired I am of bog and road,
And the crying wind and the lonesome hush!

And I am praying to God on high,
And I am praying him night and day,
For a little house, a house of my own —
Out of the wind's and the rain's way.

Padraic Colum

21   THE TERRIBLE ROBBER MEN

Oh I wish the sun was bright in the sky,
And the fox was back in his den O!
For always I'm hearing the passing by
Of the terrible robber men O!
    Of the terrible robber men.

Oh what does the fox carry over the rye,
When it's bright in the morn again O!
And what is it making the lonesome cry
With the terrible robber men O!
    With the terrible robber men.

Oh I wish the sun was bright in the sky,
And the fox was back in his den O!
For always I'm hearing the passing by
Of the terrible robber men O!
    Of the terrible robber men.

Padraic Colum

22   A DROVER

To Meath of the pastures,
From wet hills by the sea,
Through Leitrim and Longford,
Go my cattle and me.

I hear in the darkness
Their slipping and breathing —
I name them the by-ways
They're to pass without heeding;

Then the wet, winding roads,
Brown bogs with black water,
And my thoughts on white ships
And the King o' Spain's daughter.

O farmer, strong farmer!
You can spend at the fair,
But your face you must turn
To your crops and your care;

And soldiers, red soldiers!
You've seen many lands,
But you walk two by two
And by captain's commands!

O the smell of the beasts,
The wet wind in the morn,
And the proud and hard earth
Never broken for corn!

And the crowds at the fair,
The herds loosened and blind,
Loud words and dark faces,
And the wild blood behind!

(O strong men with your best
I would strive breast to breast,
I could quiet your herds
With my words, with my words!)

I will bring you, my kine,
Where there's grass to the knee,
But you'll think of scant croppings
Harsh with salt of the sea.

Padraic Colum

Along the wandering strand the sea unloads glass balls
Jellyfish, broken shells, its tangle
Of nets, cork, bits of wood,
Coral. A crooked line paid out on sand.
Here's evidence; gather it all up.

Time on window-panes
Imposes a curved edge of dust,
Hides dirt under the refrigerator, invites
The mice inside to dodge
Behind the revealing stack of empty bottles.
In the refrigerator the ice is growing
Into odd shapes; outside
The house, the cracks are spreading
In the asphalt; they reach out, join
To weave some kind of message.

Age creates
People whose wrinkles betray
How they smiled, with scars
Of operations. They have white patches
Where the sun has not reached them:
The skin grows hard on their hands;
Some of them have false teeth.
The flick of their lashes, the flutter of their shirtfronts
Is evidence of life.

Eiléan Ni Chuilleanáin

24 CHORUS OF SPIRITS

Gently! — gently! — down! — down!
   From the starry courts on high,
Gently step adown, down
   The ladder of the sky.

Sunbeam steps are strong enough
   For such airy feet:
Spirits, blow your trumpets rough,
   So as they be sweet!

Breathe them loud, the Queen descending,
   Yet a lowly welcome breathe,
Like so many flowerets bending
   Zepher's breezy foot beneath.

George Darley

25 LAMENT FOR THE DEATH
OF EOGHAN RUADH O'NEILL

(Time: 10 November 1649.
Place: Ormond's Camp, Co. Waterford.)

'Did they dare, did they dare, to slay Eoghan Ruadh
   O'Neill?'
'Yes, they slew with poison him they feared to meet
   with steel.'
'May God wither up their hearts! May their blood
   cease to flow!
May they walk in living death, who poisoned
   Eoghan Ruadh!'

'Though it break my heart to hear, say again the
    bitter words.'
'From Derry, against Cromwell, he marched to
    measure swords;
But the weapon of the Saxon met him on his way,
And he died at Cloch Uachtar, upon Saint
    Leonard's day.'

'Sagest in the council was he, kindest in the Hall:
Sure we never won a battle — 'twas Eoghan
    won them all.
Had he lived — had he lived — our dear country
    had been free;
But he's dead, but he's dead, and 'tis slaves
    we'll ever be.

'O'Farrell and Clanricarde, Preston and Red Hugh,
Audley and MacMahon — ye are valiant, wise and
    true;
But — what, what are ye all to our darling
    who is gone?
The Rudder of our ship was he, our Castle's
    corner-stone!

'We thought you would not die — we were sure
    you would not go,
And leave us in our utmost need to Cromwell's
    cruel blow —
Sheep without a shepherd, when the snow
    shuts out the sky —
Oh! why did you leave us, Eoghan?
    Why did you die?

Thomas Davis

Does any man dream that a Gael can fear?
    Of a thousand deeds let him learn but one!
The Shannon swept onward, broad and clear,
    Between the leaguers and worn Athlone.

"Break down the bridge!" Six warriors rushed
    Thro' the storm of shot and the storm of shell;
With late, but certain, victory flushed,
    The grim Dutch gunners eyed them well.

They wrenched at the planks 'mid a hail of fire:
    They fell in death, their work half done;
The bridge stood fast; and nigh and nigher
    The foe swarmed darkly, densely on:

"Oh, who for Erin will strike a stroke?
    Who hurl yon planks where the waters roar?"
Six warriors forth from their comrades broke,
    And flung them upon that bridge once more.

Again at the rocking planks they dashed;
    And four dropped dead, and two remained;
The huge beams groaned, and the arch down-crashed;
    Two stalwart swimmers the margin gained.

St. Ruth in his stirrups stood up and cried,
    "I have seen no deed like that in France!"
With a toss of his head Sarsfield replied,
    "They had luck, the dogs! 'Twas a merry chance!"

Oh! many a year, upon Shannon's side,
    They sang upon moor, and they sang upon heath,
Of the twain that breasted that raging tide,
    And the ten that shook bloody hands with death.

Aubrey de Vere

43

27 THE MARCH TO KINSALE
(December, 1601)

O'er many a river bridged with ice,
    Through many a vale with snow-drifts dumb,
Past quaking fen and precipice
    The Princes of the North are come!

Lo, these are they that year by year
    Roll'd back the tide of England's war; —
Rejoice, Kinsale! thy help is near!
    That wondrous winter march is o'er.

    And thus they sang, 'Tomorrow morn
    Our eyes shall rest upon the foe:
    Roll on, swift night, in silence borne,
    And blow, thou breeze of sunrise, blow!'

Blithe as a boy on marched the host,
    With droning pipe and clear-voiced harp;
At last above that southern coast
    Rang out their war-steeds' whinny sharp:
And up the sea-salt slopes they wound,
    And airs once more of ocean quaff'd;
Those frosty woods the rocks that crown'd
    As though May touched them, waved and laugh'd.

    And thus they sang,'Tomorrow morn
    Our eyes shall rest upon our foe:
    Roll on, swift night, in silence borne,
    And blow, thou breeze of sunrise, blow!'

Beside their watchfires couch'd all night
    Some slept, some laugh'd, at cards some play'd,
While, chaunting on a central height
    Of moonlit crag, the priesthood pray'd:
And some to sweetheart, some to wife
    Sent message kind; while others told
Triumphant tales of recent fight,
    Or legends of their sires of old.

    And thus they sang, 'Tomorrow morn
    Our eyes at last shall see the foe:
    Roll on, swift night, in silence borne,
    And blow, thou breeze of sunrise, blow!'

Aubrey De Vere

28 BOY BATHING

On the edge of the springboard
A boy poses, columned light
Poised.
Seagull's crying wrinkles
The brown parchment cliffs.
His body shines: a knife!
Spread wings, he opens
Plunges
Through the gold glass of sunshine
Smashes
In crumbs of glass the silence.

Denis Devlin

29   THE SCARECROW

One shoulder up, the other down,
His hat upon a broomstick crown,
I saw a ragged scarecrow stand,
Guarding the sown and sunlit land.

Awhile I stood, and not a crow
Near the rich furrows dared to go.
But when I turned away, why then
They fell to work like husbandmen.

H. L. Doak

30   STILL LIFE WITH ASHTRAY

After the short few hours its morning bowl
was littered with a surprising collection of butts

stubbed and twisted they lay, mute arguments,
as if the light that had burned to each was a life, forced
out among the ash and charred matches.

Beside them in primary colours, the matchbox
which clattered emptily like a toy when i shook it.

The two chairs were still pulled out as if someone had just left.

Smoke.

A packet of cigarettes forgotten on the mantlepiece.

Desmond Egan

31 THE FLY IN THE TOWER

was a thorn of noise
in from the river bzz banging my lamp
irritating bzz desperate
as if the room were a web
BZZ
inviting outrage
like an autumn wasp —

so that i left the chair
i left the desk, lashing out
and AGAIN
hardly feeling the hit

but the fly
had skidded into a wall
and fallen and folded, a
spot on the quilt

Desmond Egan

32 THE PETS

Colm had a cat,
and a wren,
and a fly.

The cat was a pet,
and the wren,
and the fly.

And it happened that the wren
ate the fly;
and it happened that the cat
ate the wren.

Then the cat died.

So Saint Colm lacked a cat
and a wren,
and a fly.

But Saint Colm loved the cat,
and the wren,
and the fly,

so he prayed to get them back,
cat and wren;
and he prayed to get them back,
wren and fly.

And the cat became alive
and delivered up the wren;
and the wren became alive
and delivered up the fly;
and they all lived with Colm
till the day came to die.

First the cat died.
Then the wren died.
Then the fly.

Robert Farren

33 LAMENT FOR THE DEATH
   OF THOMAS DAVIS

I walked through Ballinderry in the springtime,
   When the bud was on the tree,
And I said, in every fresh-ploughed field beholding
   The sowers striding free,
Scattering broadcast forth the corn in golden plenty,
   On the quick, seed-clasping soil,
Even such this day among the fresh-stirred hearts of Erin
   Thomas Davis, is thy toil!

I sat by Ballyshannon in the summer,
   And saw the salmon leap,
And I said, as I beheld the gallant creatures
   Spring glittering from the deep,
Through the spray and through the prone heaps
      striving onward
   To the calm, clear streams above,
So seekest thou thy native founts of freedom, Thomas Davis,
   In thy brightness of strength and love!

I stood on Derrybawn in the autumn,
   I heard the eagle call,
With a clangorous cry of wrath and lamentation
   That filled the wide mountain hall,
O'er the bare, deserted place of his plundered eyrie,
And I said, as he screamed and soared,
So callest thou, thou wrathful-soaring Thomas Davis,
For a nation's rights restored.

O brave young men, my love, my pride, my promise,
    'Tis on you my hopes are set,
In manliness, in kindliness, in justice,
    To make Erin a nation yet;
Self-respecting, self-relying, self-advancing,
    In union or in severance, free and strong,
And if God grants this, then, under God, to Thomas Davis
    Let the greater praise belong!

Samuel Ferguson

34 THE CRAB TREE

Here is the Crab-tree,
Firm and erect,
In spite of the thin soil
In spite of neglect.
The twisted root grapples
For sap with the rock,
And draws the hard juice
To the succulent top:
Here are wild apples,
Here's a tart crop!

Oliver Gogarty

35   GOLDEN STOCKINGS

Golden stockings you had on
In the meadow where you ran;
And your little knees together
Bobbed like pippins in the weather
When the breezes rush and fight
For those dimples of delight;
And they dance from the pursuit,
And the leaf looks like the fruit.

I have many a sight in mind
That would last if I were blind;
Many verses I could write
That would bring me many a sight.
Now I only see but one,
See you running in the sun;
And the gold-dust coming up
From the trampled butter-cup.

Oliver Gogarty

36 GALWAY

A grey town in a country bare,
The leaden seas between,
When light falls on the hills of Clare
And shows their valleys green:
Take in my heart your place again
Between your lake and sea,
O City of the watery plain
That means so much to me!

Your cut-stone houses row on row,
Your streams too deep to sing,
Whose waters shine with green as though
They had disolved the Spring:
Your streets that still bring into view
The harbour and its spars;
The chimneys with the turf-smoke blue
That never hides the stars!

It is not very long since you,
For Memory is long,
Saw her I owe my being to,
And heart that takes to song,
Walk with a row of laughing girls
From Salthill to Eyre Square,
Light from the water on their curls
That never lit more fair.

Again may come your glorious days,
Your ships come back to port,
And to your city's shining ways
The Spanish dames resort!
And ere the tidal water falls
Your ships put out to sea . . .
Like crimson roses in grey walls
Your memories to me!

Oliver Gogarty

Beside yon straggling fence that skirts the way,
With blossom'd furze unprofitably gay,
There, in his noisy mansion, skilled to rule,
The village master taught his little school.
A man severe he was, and stern to view;
I knew him well, and every truant knew:
Well had the boding tremblers learned to trace
The day's disasters in his morning face;
Full well they laughed with counterfeited glee
At all his jokes, for many a joke had he;
Full well the busy whisper circling round
Conveyed the dismal tidings when he frowned.
Yet he was kind, or, if severe in aught,
The love he bore to learning was in fault;
The village all declared how much he knew:
'Twas certain he could write, and cypher too;
Lands he could measure, terms and tides presage,
And e'en the story ran that he could guage:
In arguing, too, the parson owned his skill;
For e'en though vanquished, he could argue still;
While words of learned length and thundering sound
Amazed the gazing rustics ranged around;
And still they gazed, and still the wonder grew,
That one small head could carry all he knew.

But past is all his fame. The very spot
Where many a time he triumphed, is forgot.

Oliver Goldsmith

The grand road from the mountain goes shining to the sea,
    And there is traffic in it and many a horse and cart,
But the little roads of Cloonagh are dearer far to me,
    And the little roads of Cloonagh go rambling through
        my heart.

A great storm from the ocean goes shouting o'er the hill,
    And there is glory in it and terror on the wind,
But the haunted air of twilight is very strange and still,
    And the little winds of twilight are dearer to my mind.

The great waves of the Atlantic sweep storming on the way,
    Shining green and silver with the hidden herring shoal,
But the Little Waves of Breffny have drenched my heart
      in spray,
    And the Little Waves of Breffny go stumbling through
        my soul.

Eva Gore-Booth

Let all the fish that swim the sea —
    Salmon and turbot, cod and ling —
Bow down the head and bend the knee
    To herring, their king! — to herring, their king!
    Sing, Thugamar fein an samhradh linn,
    'Tis we have brought the summer in.

The sun sank down, so round and red,
    Upon the bay, upon the bay;
The sails shook idly overhead —
    Becalmed we lay, becalmed we lay.
    Sing, Thugamar fein an samhradh linn,
    'Tis we have brought the summer in.

Till Shaun, 'The Eagle', dropped on deck,
    The bright-eyed boy, the bright-eyed boy;
'Tis he has spied your silver track,
    Herring, our joy — herring, our joy.
    Sing, Thugamar fein an samhradh linn,
    'Tis we have brought the summer in.

It was in with the sails and away to the shore,
    With the rise and swing, the rise and swing
Of two stout lads at each smoking oar,
    After herring, our king — herring, our king.
    Sing, Thugamar fein an samhradh linn,
    'Tis we have brought the summer in.

The Manx and the Cornish raised the shout,
    And joined the chase, and joined the chase;
But their fleets they fouled as they went about,
    And we won the race, we won the race.
    Sing, Thugamar fein an samhradh linn,
    'Tis we have brought the summer in.

For we turned and faced you full to land,
    Down the goleen long, the goleen long,
And after you slipped from strand to strand
    Our nets so strong, our nets so strong.
    Sing, Thugamar fein an samhradh linn,
    'Tis we have brought the summer in.

Then we called to our sweethearts and our wives:
    'Come welcome us home — welcome us home!
'Till they ran to meet us for their lives
    Into the foam, into the foam.
    Sing, Thugamar fein an samhradh linn,
    'Tis we have brought the summer in.

Oh, the kissing of hands and waving of caps
    From girl and boy, from girl and boy,
While you leapt by scores in the lasses' laps,
    Herring, our pride and joy.
    Sing, Thugamar fein an samhradh linn,
    'Tis we have brought the summer in.

Alfred P. Graves

whom I ask for no gift
whom I thank for all things,
this is the Morning.
night is gone, a dawn
comes up in birds and sounds of the city.
there will be light
to live by, things
to see: my eyes will lift
to where the sun in vermillion sits,
and I will love and have pity.

Michael Hartnett

the night before Patricia's funeral in 1951,
I stayed up late talking to my father.

how goes the night, boy?
          the moon is down:
          dark is the town
          in this nightfall.
how goes the night, boy?
          soon is her funeral,
          her small white burial.
she was my threeyears child,
her honey hair, her eyes
small ovals of thrush-eggs.
how goes the night, boy?
          it is late: lace
          at the window
          blows back in the wind.
how goes the night, boy?
          — Oh, my poor white fawn!
how goes the night, boy?
          it is dawn.

Michael Hartnett

The pockets of our great coats full of barley —
No kitchens on the run, no striking camp —
We moved quick and sudden in our own country.
The priest lay behind ditches with the tramp.
A people, hardly marching — on the hike —
We found new tactics happening each day:
We'd cut through reins and rider with the pike
And stampede cattle into infantry,
Then retreat through hedges where cavalry must be
    thrown.
Until, on Vinegar Hill, the fatal conclave.
Terraced thousands died, shaking scythes at cannon.
The hillside blushed, soaked in our broken wave.
They buried us without shroud or coffin
And in August the barley grew up out of the grave.

Seamus Heaney

Cut from the green hedge a forked hazel stick
That he held tight by the arms of the V:
Circling the terrain, hunting the pluck
Of water, nervous, but professionally

Unfussed. The pluck came sharp as a sting.
The rod jerked down with precise convulsions,
Spring water suddenly broadcasting
Through a green aerial its secret stations.

The bystanders would ask to have a try.
He handed them the rod without a word.
It lay dead in their grasp till nonchalantly
He gripped expectant wrists. The hazel stirred.

Seamus Heaney

44   THATCHER

Bespoke for weeks, he turned up some morning
Unexpectedly, his bicycle slung
With a light ladder and a bag of knives.
He eyed the old rigging, poked at the eaves,

Opened and handled sheaves of lashed wheat-straw.
Next, the bundled rods: hazel and willow
Were flicked for weight, twisted in case they'd snap.
It seemed he spent the morning warming up:

Then fixed the ladder, laid out well honed blades
And snipped at straw and sharpened ends of rods
That, bent in two, made a white-pronged staple
For pinning down his world, handful by handful.

Couchant for days on sods above the rafters
He shaved and flushed the butts, stitched all together
Into a sloped honeycomb, a stubble patch,
And left them gaping at his Midas touch.

Seamus Heaney

45 THE FORGE

All I know is a door into the dark.
Outside, old axles and iron hoops rusting;
Inside, the hammered anvil's short-pitched ring,
The unpredictable fantail of sparks
Or hiss when a new shoe toughens in water.
The anvil must be somewhere in the centre,
Horned as a unicorn, at one end square,
Set there immoveable: an altar
Where he expends himself in shape and music.
Sometimes, leather-aproned, hairs in his nose,
He leans out on the jamb, recalls a clatter
Of hoofs where traffic is flashing in rows;
Then grunts and goes in, with a slam and flick
To beat real iron out, to work the bellows.

Seamus Heaney

All year round the whin
Can show a blossom or two
But it's in full bloom now.
As if the small yolk stain

From all the birds' eggs in
All the nests of the spring
Were spiked and hung
Everywhere on bushes to ripen.

Hills oxidize gold.
Above the smoulder of green shoot
And dross of dead thorns underfoot
The blossoms scald.

Put a match under
Whins, they go up of a sudden.
They make no flame in the sun
But a fierce heat tremor

Yet incineration like that
Only takes the thorn.
The tough sticks don't burn,
Remain like bone, charred horn.

Gilt, jaggy, springy, frilled
This stunted, dry richness
Persists on hills, near stone ditches,
Over flintbed and battlefield.

Seamus Heaney

47 LOAD

Today we carted home the last brown sheaf
and hookt the scythe agenst the dry barn wall:
the yellow border's on the chestnut leaf,
the beech leaf's yellow all.

Tomorrow we must bring the apples in,
they are as big as they shall ever be:
already starlings eager to begin
have tasted many a tree.

And in the garden, all the roses done,
the light lies gently, faint and almost cold,
on wither'd goldenrod and snapdragon
and tarnisht marigold.

John Hewitt

48 GRACE BEFORE BEER

For what this house affords us,
Come, praise the brewer most —
Who caught into a bottle
The barley's gentle ghost —
Until our parching throttles
In silence we employ —
Like geese that drink a mouthful,
Then stretch their necks with joy!

F. R. Higgins

49   DOTAGE

If I go by many a sloe bush
    Or crab tree from Renvyle,
In Kylemore or Clifden
    I'll lay my bones awhile,
Where the dawn may bloom above me
    In a bush of dark red bells,
And the mouth may break its fasting
    On the cress of twenty wells.

But the windy gaps of Twelve Pins
    Lie bare before my gaze;
And the roads I've got to hobble
    Are full of lonesome days —
With only a dream of those blue lips
    Gobbling a foolish wine
From the cups of Grace O'Maille,
    When Spanish sails were mine.

Or when the bold Armada
    Rode golden long ago,
Through clean waves plumbed with
        brightness
    To the sun-washed rocks below;
There every man's chest of treasure
    Was a cask of sack and a gun,
Until his full sailed castle
    Blazed down in a terrible sun.

O I'll go by many a sloe bush
    Or crab tree from Renvyle,
And in Kylemore or Clifden
    I'll lay my bones awhile,
Passing an eve of Bealtaine
    Within a friendly door,
While many brave shoes of music
    Shake laughter on the floor.

F. R. Higgins

A lone grey heron is flying, flying
　　Home to her nest,
And over the rush-blown waters
　　Burning in the west,
Where an orange moon is lying
　　Softly on soft air,
As the dusk comes lounging after
　　Sleepy care.

Ah, now that heron is slowly, slowly
　　Plying her wing,
But soon she'll droop to the rushes
　　Where the winds swing;
She'll stand in the pools and coldly
　　Dream on the sly,
With her wild eyes watching the fishes,
　　As stars watch you from on high.

F. R. Higgins

His last days linger in that low attic
That barely lets out the night,
With its gabled window on Knackers' Alley,
Just hoodwinking the light.

He comes and goes by that gabled window
And then on the window pane
He leans, as thin as a bottled shadow —
A look and he's gone again:

Eyeing, maybe, some fine fish-women
In the best shawls of the Coombe
Or, maybe, the knife-grinder plying his treadle,
A run of sparks from his thumb!

But, O you should see him gazing, gazing,
When solemnly out on the road
The horse-drays pass overladen with grasses,
Each driver lost in his load;

Gazing until they return; and suddenly,
As galloping by they race,
From his pale eyes, like glass breaking,
Light leaps on his face.

F. R. Higgins

The sunflower bows upon her breast
Her golden head, and goes to rest
Forgetting all the days that were
When she was young and proud and fair
And in the glowing August air
Bees came and sought and found her sweet.

Now earth is cold about her feet,
And wasps forsake her, and the sun
No longer seeks her for the one
Flower in his splendid image made
Her beauty's done, her farewell said.

Her large leaves fold in weary wise,
And heavy are her great brown eyes.
The living rubies that would run
Across her discs that mocked the sun —
The ladybirds — sleep everyone.

The great stalk stoops towards the earth
Where all dreams end, whence all birth.
The hive-bee has forgotton quite
How once he loved her, for the night
Has come wherein no bee can spy
Sweet in this flower dead and dry.

Nora Hopper

53 THE TOY HORSE

Somebody, when I was young, stole my toy horse,
The charm of my morning romps, my man's delight.
For two days I grieved, holding my sorrow like flowers
Between the bars of my sullen angry mind.

Next day I went out with evil in my heart,
Evil between my eyes and at the tips of my hands,
Looking for my enemy at the armed stations,
Until I found him, playing in his garden

With my toy horse, urgent in the battle
Against the enemies of his Unreason's land:
He was so happy, I gave him also
My vivid coloured crayons and my big glass marble.

Valentin Iremonger

54 SAINT FIACRE

Kind Saint! who loved the garden
        flowers,
Be not unmindful of the hours
Spent in unremitting toil
To trim the hedges, break the soil,
And work with clippers, trowels, or
        rakes
Until every muscle aches.

May the slips and bulbs and seeds
Grow more bountiful, rank weeds
Be eaten up when summer brings
Snails, and flies, and creepy things,
And let the borders and the shrubs
Be colourful, and free from grubs.

John Irvine

The night is on the dark sea wave
And the boats are on the deep,
But here within the quiet room
My treasure lies asleep.
Oh! may Our Lady come and bless
The cradle where you lie,
And wind and wave, and moon and
    stars,
Shall sing you lullaby.

The woodland birds are silent now,
And the empty fields are still.
Night in her sable vestment walks
Across the lonely hill.
Oh! may Our Lady stoop to rock
The cradle where you lie,
And wind and wave, and moon and
    stars,
Shall sing you lullaby.

John Irvine

56   GOLDENHAIR

Lean out of the window,
    Goldenhair,
I heard you singing
    A merry air.

My book is closed;
    I read no more,
Watching the fire dance
    On the floor.

I have left my book;
    I have left my room,
For I heard you singing
    Through the gloom.

Singing and singing
    A merry air,
Lean out of the window.
    Goldenhair.

James Joyce

57   THE NOISE OF WATERS

All day I hear the noise of waters
    Making moan,
Sad as the sea-bird is, when going
    Forth alone,
He hears the winds cry to the waters'
    Monotone.

The grey winds, the cold winds are blowing
    Where I go.
I hear the noise of many waters
    Far below.
All day, all night I hear them flowing
    To and fro.

James Joyce

PATRICK MAGUIRE

One day he saw a daisy and he thought it
Reminded him of his childhood —
He stopped his cart to look at it.
Was there a fairy hiding behind it?

He helped a poor woman whose cow
Had died on her;
He dragged home a drunken man on a winter's night;
And one rare moment he heard the young people playing
    on the railway stile
And he wished them happiness and whatever they most
    desired from life.

He saw the sunlight and begrudged no man
His share of what the miserly soil and soul
Gives in a season to a ploughman.
And he cried for his own loss one late night on the pillow
And yet thanked the God who had arranged these things.

Was he then a saint?
A Matt Talbot of Monaghan?

His sister Mary Anne spat poison at the children
Who sometimes came to the door selling raffle tickets
For holy funds.
'Get out, you little tramps!' she would scream
As she shook to the hens an armful of crumbs,
But Patrick often put his hand deep down
In his trouser-pocket and fingered out a penny
Or maybe a tobacco-stained caramel.
'You're soft,' said the sister; 'with other people's money
It's not a bit funny.'

The cards are shuffled and the deck
Laid flat for cutting — Tom Malone
Cut for trump. I think we'll make
This game, the last, a tanner one.
Hearts. Right. I see you're breaking
Your two-year-old. Play quick, Maguire,
The clock there says it's half-past ten —
Kate, throw another sod on that fire.
One of the card-players laughs and spits
Into the flame across a shoulder.
Outside, a noise like a rat
Among the hen-roosts. The cock crows over
The frosted townland of the night.
Eleven o'clock and still the game
Goes on and the players seem to be
Drunk in an Orient opium den.
Midnight, one o'clock, two.
Somebody's leg has fallen asleep.
What about home? Maguire, are you
Using your double-tree this week?
Why? do you want it? Play the ace.
There's it, and that's the last card for me.
A wonderful night, we had. Duffy's place
Is very convenient. Is that a ghost or a tree?
And so they go home with dragging feet
And their voices rumble like laden carts.
And they are happy as the dead or sleeping . . .
I should have led that ace of hearts.

Patrick Kavanagh

59 MY ROOM

10 by 12
And a low roof
If I stand by the side wall
My head feels the reproof.

Five holy pictures
Hang on the walls:
The Virgin and Child
St Anthony of Padua
Leo the XIII
St Patrick and the Little Flower.

My bed in the centre
So many things to me —
A dining table
A writing desk
And a slumber palace.

My room in a dusty attic
But its little window
Lets in the stars.

Patrick Kavanagh

I planted in February
A bronze-leafed beech,
In the chill brown soil
I spread out its silken fibres.

Protected it from the goats
With wire netting
And fixed it firm against
The worrying wind.

Now it is safe, I said,
April must stir
My precious baby
To greenful loveliness.

It is August now, I have hoped
But I hope no more —
My beech tree will never hide sparrows
From hungry hawks.

Patrick Kavanagh

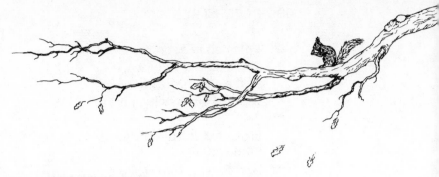

61 AUTUMN'S END

With upturned bellies lying cold
In habits black and striped with gold
Behind large windows of glass plate
Dead, swollen wasps accumulate.
Small monkeys in their Northern zoos
Grumble with unaccustomed 'flu's'.
Fat frogs harrumph and blurp in peace
On harvest bellies white as fleece
And in the wells the water's free
From beetle, bug and buzzing bee.
Soft salmon redden in the pools
And lazy squirrels shout: 'Down tools!'
Moist green leaves rest in rotting rust.
Hot donkeys roll no more in dust.

John B. Keane

62 CAOCH THE PIPER

One winter's day, long, long ago,
    When I was a little fellow,
A piper wandered to our door,
    Grey-headed, blind, and yellow:
And, oh! how glad was my young heart,
    Though earth and sky looked dreary,
To see the stranger and his dog —
    Poor 'Pinch' and Caoch O'Leary.

And when he stowed away his 'bag,'
    Crossed-barred with green and yellow,
I thought and said, 'In Ireland's ground
    There's not so fine a fellow.'
And Fineen Burke, and Shaun Magee,
    And Eily, Kate, and Mary,
Rushed in, with panting haste, to 'see'
    And 'welcome' Caoch O'Leary.

Poor Caoch and 'Pinch' slept well that night,
    And in the morning early
He called me up to hear him play
    'The wind that shakes the barley;'
And then he stroked my flaxen hair,
    And cried, 'God mark my deary!'
And how I wept when he said, 'Farewell,
    And think of Caoch O'Leary!'

Well — twenty summers had gone past,
    And June's red sun was sinking,
When I, a man, sat by my door,
    Of twenty sad things thinking.
A little dog came up the way,
    His gait was slow and weary,
And at his tail a lame man limped —
    'Twas 'Pinch' and Caoch O'Leary!

'God's blessing here!' the wanderer cried,
    'Far, far be hell's black viper;
Does any body hereabouts
    Remember Caoch the Piper?'
With swelling heart I grasped his hand;
    The old man murmured, 'Deary,
Are you the silky-headed child
    That loved poor Caoch O'Leary?'

'Yes, yes,' I said — the wanderer wept
    As if his heart was breaking —
'And where, *a vic machree* ,' he sobbed,
    'Is all the merry-making
I found here twenty years ago?'
    'My tale,' I sighed, 'might weary;
Enough to say — there's none but me
    To welcome Caoch O'Leary.'

'Vo, vo, vo!' the old man cried,
    And wrung his hands in sorrow,
'Pray let me in, *astore machree,*
    And I'll *go home* to-morrow.
My 'peace is made;' I'll calmly leave
    This world so cold and dreary;
And you shall keep my pipes and dog,
    And pray for Caoch O'Leary.'

With 'Pinch' I watched his bed that night;
    Next day his wish was granted:
He died; and Father James was brought,
    And the Requiem Mass was chanted.
The neighbours came; we dug his grave
    Near Eily, Kate, and Mary,
And there he sleeps his last sweet sleep.
    God rest you! Caoch O'Leary.

John Keegan

Getting up early promises well:
A milkhorse on the road
Induces thoughts of a sleeping world
And a waking God.

This hour has something sacred;
Bells will be ringing soon,
But now I am content to watch
The day begin to bloom.

I would only waste my breath
On poor superfluous words;
How perfectly they sing for me —
The new invisible birds

Who celebrate the light that spreads
Like love to window sills,
As morning steps like a laughing girl
Down from the Dublin hills.

Brendan Kennelly

64   SEA

I am patient, repetitive, multi-voiced,
Yet few hear me
And fewer still trouble to understand

Why, for example, I caress
And hammer the land.
I do not brag of my depths

Or my currents, I do not
Boast of my moods or my colours
Or my breath in your thought.

In time I surrender my drowned,
My appetite speaks for itself,
I could swallow all you have found

And open for more,
My green tongues licking the shores
Of the world

Like starved beasts reaching for men
Who will not understand
When I rage and roar

When I bellow and threaten
I am obeying a law
Observing a discipline.

This is the rhythm
I live.
This is the reason I move

In hunger and skill
To give you the pick of my creatures.
This is why I am willing to kill,

Chill every created nerve.
You have made me a savage master
Because I know how to serve.

Brendan Kennelly

65   GIRL IN A ROPE

By the still canal
She enters a slack rope,
Moves, slowly at first, round and round;
Gathering speed,
(Faster, faster now)
She clips the air without a sound —
Swift whirling sight,
Creator of a high design,
Orbiting in sheer delight
The red and white No Parking sign.

Brendan Kennelly

And will the flowers die?

And will the people die?

And every day do you grow old, do I
grow old, no I'm not old, do
flowers grow old?

Old things - do you throw them out?

Do you throw old people out?

And how you know a flower that's old?

The petals fall, the petals fall from flowers,
and do the petals fall from people too,
every day more petals fall until the
floor where I would like to play I
want to play is covered with old
flowers and people all the same
together lying there with petals fallen
on the dirty floor I want to play
the floor you come and sweep
with the huge broom.

The dirt you sweep, what happens that,
what happens all the dirt you sweep
from flowers and people, what
happens all the dirt? Is all the
dirt what's left of flowers and
people, all the dirt there in a
heap under the huge broom that
sweeps everything away?

Why you work so hard, why brush
and sweep to make a heap of dirt?

And who will bring new flowers?

And who will bring new people? Who will
bring new flowers to put in water
where no petals fall on to the
floor where I would like to
play? Who will bring new flowers
that will not hang their heads
like tired old people wanting sleep?
Who will bring new flowers that
do not split and shrivel every
day? And if we have new flowers,
will we have new people too to
keep the flowers alive and give
them water?

And will the new young flowers die?

And will the new young people die?

And why?

Brendan Kennelly

67   LIGHTNING

At a decent distance
From the heads of men
I happen

And am gone.
This is how
I light up heaven

And define the dark.
You think I must
Be something of an exhibitionist,

A dramatic braggart of light?
I am a mere moment
Between this and that

Yet so much that moment
I
Illumine the sky

And the small homes of men,
Flash through their fears, spotlight their joys.
My deepest nature is quiet and private.
I cannot escape the noise.

Brendan Kennelly

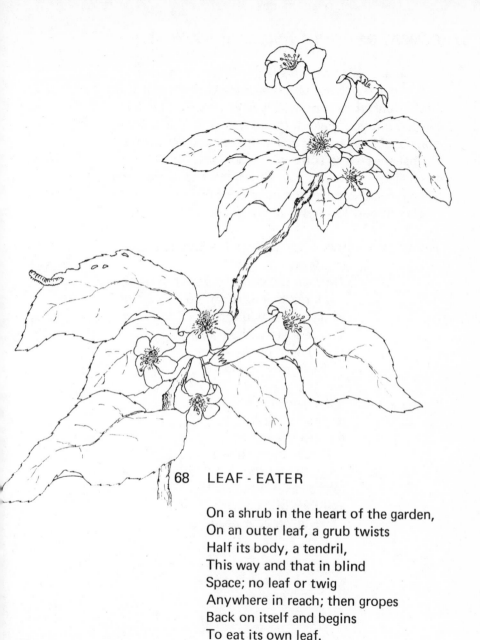

68   LEAF - EATER

On a shrub in the heart of the garden,
On an outer leaf, a grub twists
Half its body, a tendril,
This way and that in blind
Space; no leaf or twig
Anywhere in reach; then gropes
Back on itself and begins
To eat its own leaf.

Thomas Kinsella

'You are welcome, Cúchulainn.'

'I could trust your welcome once.' Cúchulainn said.
'But I don't trust it now. Anyway,' he said, 'it is for
me and not you, Ferdia, to bid welcome: this is my
homeland, you are the intruder. And you are wrong
to challenge me to combat. It would suit me better
to challenge you: you have driven out our women and
young men and boys, and our troops of horses, our
herds and our flocks and all our goods.'

Ferdia: 'What brings you here, Squinter,
to try my strength!
Through the steam of your horses
   I'll reach and redden you.
You'll regret you came.
You're a fire without fuel.
You'll need plenty of help
   if you ever see home.'

Cúchulainn: 'Like a great boar
before his herd,
I'll overwhelm you
   before these armies.
I'll push you and punish you
to the last of your skill,
and then bring down
   havoc on your head!'

Ferdia: 'It is I who will kill,
                 I who will destroy,
                 I who will drive
                     Ulster's hero to flight
                 before all eyes.
                 By my doing
                 they'll rue their loss
                     early and late.'

Cúchulainn: 'Must we start our fight
                 groaning over corpses?
                 Come what may
                     let us enter the ford
                 to meet death before the hosts
                 with bloody spear-blade
                 or the savage sword
                     if our time is come.'

He spoke further and Ferdia listened:

'Ferdia son of Damán,
noble warrior, do not come.
You will suffer more than me
and bring sorrow to your company.

Do not come — and in the wrong —
or here you'll find your resting-place.
How can it be that you alone
could escape my fatal rage?

'Fast friends, forest-companions,
we made one bed and slept one sleep
in foreign lands after the fray.
Scáthach's pupils, two together,
we'd set forth to comb the forest.'

Ferdia said:

'Cúchulainn, you bear your cunning lightly,
but I have mastered the same trade.
Our friendship is finished, through foul play.
Prepare to face your first defeat.
Forget that we were foster-brothers.
Squinter, you are past help!'

(They fight in the ford for three days. On the third
day, Cúchulainn, casting it with his right foot, wounds
Ferdia fatally with *gae bolga,* a terrible weapon that
entered the victim's body with a single wound, then
opened into thirty barbs.)

'That is enough now,' Ferdia said, 'I'll die of that.
There is strength in the thrust of your right foot. It is
wrong I should fall at your hand.'
He said:

> 'Hound of the bright deeds,
> you have killed me unfairly.
> Your guilt clings to me
> as my blood sticks to you.
>
> By the way of deceit
> no good can come.
> I am struck dumb.
> I am leaving this life.
>
> My ribs are crushed in,
> my heart is all blood.
> I have not fought well.
> Hound, I am fallen.'

Cúchulainn ran toward him and clasped his two arms
round him and carried him — weapons, armour and
harness — north across the ford with him.

At last, Cúchulainn's charioteer spoke:
'Well, Cúcuc,' Laeg said, 'Let us leave the ford now.
We have been here too long.'

'Very well, let us leave it, friend Laeg,' Cúchulainn
said. 'All the struggles and contests that I ever fought
seem only playful games now after my struggle with
Ferdia.'

And Cúchulainn said these words:

> 'It was all play, all sport,
> until Ferdia came to the ford.
> A like learning we both had,
> the same rights, the same belongings,
> the same good foster-mother
> — her whose name is most honoured.
>
> All play, all sport,
> until Ferdia came to the ford.
> The same force and fury we had,
> the same feats of war also.
> Scáthach awarded two shields,
> one to me, one to Ferdia.
>
> All play, all sport,
> until Ferdia came to the ford.
>
> Misery! A pillar of gold
> I have levelled in the ford,
> the bull of the tribe-herd,
> braver than any man.
>
> All play, all sport,
> until Ferdia came to the ford
> — fiery and ferocious lion,
> fatal, furious flood-wave!

All play, all sport,
until Ferdia came to the ford.
I thought beloved Ferdia
would live forever after me
— yesterday, a mountain-side;
today, nothing but a shade.

I have slaughtered, on this Táin,
three countless multitudes:
choice cattle, choice men,
and horses, fallen everywhere!

The army, a huge multitude,
that came from cruel Cruachan
has lost between a half and a third,
slaughtered in my savage sport.

Never came to the battle-field.
nor did Banba's belly bear,
nor over sea or land came
a king's son of fairer fame.'

Thomas Kinsella (from the Táin)

70 DICK KING

In your ghost, Dick King, in your phantom vowels I read
That death roves our memories igniting
Love. Kind plague, low voice in a stubbled throat,
You haunt with the taint of age and of vanished good,
Fouling my thought with losses.

Clearly now I remember rain on the cobbles,
Ripples in the iron trough, and the horses' dipped
Faces under the Fountain in James's Street,
When I sheltered my nine years against your buttons
And your own dread years were to come;

And your voice, in a pause of softness, named the dead,
Hushed as though the city had died by fire,
Bemused . . . discovering, discovering
A gate to enter temperate ghosthood by;
And I squeezed your fingers till you found again
My hand hidden in yours.
                              I squeeze your fingers:

Dick King was an upright man.
Sixty years he trod
The dull stations underfoot.
Fifteen he lies with God.

By the salt seaboard he grew up
But left its rock and rain
To bring a dying language east
And dwell in Basin Lane.

By the Southern Railway he increased:
His second soul was born
In the clangour of the iron sheds,
The hush of the late horn.

An invalid he took to wife.
She prayed her life away;
Her whisper filled the whitewashed yard
Until her dying day.

And season in, season out,
He made his wintry bed.
He took the path to the turnstile
Morning and night till he was dead.

He clasped his hands in a Union ward
To hear St. James's bell.
I searched his eyes though I was young,
The last to wish him well.

Thomas Kinsella

71 TARA

The mist hung on the slope, growing whiter
On the thin grass and dung by the mounds;
It hesitated at the dyke, among briars.

Our children picked up the wrapped flasks, capes and baskets
And we trailed downward among whins and thrones
In a muffled dream, guided by slender axe-shapes.

Our steps scattered on the soft turf, leaving
No trace, the childrens' voices like light.
Low in the sky behind us, a vast silver shield

Seethed and consumed itself in the thick ether.
A horse appeared at the rampart like a ghost,
And tossed his neck at ease, with a hint of harness.

Thomas Kinsella

96

There's famine in the land, its grip is tightening
   still,
There's trouble, black and bitter, on every side I
   glance,
There are dead upon the roadside, and dead upon
   the hill,
But my Jamie's safe and well away in France,
   Happy France,
In the far-off, gay and gallant land of France.

The sea sobs to the grey shore, the grey shore to
   the sea,
Men meet and greet, and part again as in some
   evil trance,
There's a bitter blight upon us, as plain as plain
   can be,
But my Jamie's safe and well away in France,
   Happy France,
In the far-off, gay and gallant land of France.

Oh not for all the coined gold that ever I could
   name
Would I bring you back, my Jamie, from your
   song and feast and dance,
Would I bring you to the hunger, the weariness
   and shame,
Would I bring you back to Clare out of France,
   Happy France,
In the far-off, gay and gallant land of France.

I'm no great sleeper now, for the nights are cruel
    cold,
And if there be a bit of sup 'tis by some friendly
    chance,
But I keep my heart warm, and I keep my
    courage bold
By thinking of my Jamie safe in France,
    Happy France,
In the far-off, gay and gallant land of France.

Emily Lawless

73   A DREAM DANCE

Maeve held a ball on the dún,
Cuculain and Eimer were there,
In the light of an old broken moon
I was dancing with Deirdre the fair

How loud was the laughter of Finn
As he blundered about thro' a reel,
Tripping up Caoilte the thin,
Or jostling the dreamy Aleel.

And when the dance ceased for a song,
How sweet was the singing of Fand,
We could hear her far, wandering along,
My hand in that beautiful hand.

Francis Ledwidge

Every night at Currabwee
Little men with leather hats
Mend the boots of Faery
From the tough wings of the bats.
So my mother told to me,
And she is wise you will agree.

Louder than a cricket's wing
All night long their hammer's glee
Times the merry songs they sing
Of Ireland glorious and free.
So I heard Joseph Plunkett say,
You know he heard them but last May.

And when the night is very cold
They warm their hands against the light
Of stars that make the waters gold
Where they are labouring all the night.
So Pearse said, and he knew the truth,
Among the stars he spent his youth.

And I, myself, have often heard
Their singing as the stars went by,
For am I not of those who reared
The banner of old Ireland high,
From Dublin town to Turkey's shores,
And where the Vardar loudly roars?

Francis Ledwidge

75 BOYS

I do be thinking God must laugh
The time He makes a boy;
All element the creatures are,
And divilmint and joy.
Careless and gay as a wad in a window,
Swift as a redshanks, and wild as a hare;
Heartscalds and torments — but sorra a mother
Has got one to spare.

Winifred M. Letts

76 A SOFT DAY

A soft day, thank God!
A wind from the south
With a honeyed mouth;
A scent of drenching leaves,
Briar and beech and lime,
White elder-flower and thyme
And the soaking grass smells sweet,
Crushed by my two bare feet,
While the rain drips,
Drips, drips, drips from the eaves.

A soft day, thank God!
The hills wear a shroud
Of silver cloud;
The web the spider weaves
Is a glittering net;
The woodland path is wet,
And the soaking earth smells sweet
Under my two bare feet,
And the rain drips,
Drips, drips, drips from the leaves.

Winifred M. Letts

Spring, the Travelling Man, has been here,
    Here in the glen;
He must have passed by in the grey of the dawn,
    When only the robin and wren
    Were awake,
Watching out with their bright little eyes
    In the midst of the brake.
    The rabbits, maybe, heard him pass,
    Stepping light on the grass,
Whistling careless and gay at the break o' the day.
    Then the blackthorn to give him delight
    Put on raiment of white:
    And, all for his sake,
    The gorse on the hill, where he rested an hour,
    Grew bright with a splendour of flower.
    My grief, that I was not aware
    Of himself being there;
    It is I would have given my dower
    To have seen him set forth,
Whistling careless and gay in the grey of the morn,
By gorse bush and fraughan and thorn,
    On his way to the north.

Winifred M. Letts

Pushing the wedge of his body
Between cromlech and stone circle,
He excavates down mine shafts
And back into the depths of the hill.

His path straight and narrow
And not like the fox's zig-zags,
The arc of the hare who leaves
A silhouette on the sky line.

Night's silence around his shoulders,
His face lit by the moon, he
Manages the earth with his paws,
Returns underground to die.

Michael Longley

When God created water He must have thought of fish
And said, 'Let there be salmon to lie on Adam's dish!'
So he created Adam, for salmon must be caught
And flies too he created, and then of rods He thought;
So trees grew straight and slender, and Adam learned to fish
And thanked the Lord each evening for the brightness on
     his dish.

But who created bailiffs in a dark hour of the night?
Not God, Who loves good fellows and taught fish how to
     bite;
Not God Who has created the peaceful flowing stream.
The salmon ripe for taking when he leaps for joy in Spring.

A wise man, Fionn Mac Cumhaill, caught a salmon for his
     tea
That lived on nuts of knowledge, dropped from a knowing
     tree;
He cooked it and he tasted and knew all men could wish
And wise men ever since then sit by a stream and fish;
But men unwise and evil, prompted by vicious greed,
Forbid good men their pleasure in doing this good deed.

Let others praise the herring, the tunny, trout or whale,
Give me the noble salmon with lightning in his tail;
To monarchs leave the sturgeon, the carp of golden hue —
I'll snare the silver salmon, and share the dish with you.

Donagh MacDonagh

I dreamt last night of you, John-John,
    And thought you called to me;
And when I woke this morning, John,
    Yourself I hoped to see;
But I was all alone, John-John,
    Though still I heard your call:
I put my boots and bonnet on,
    And took my Sunday shawl,
And went, full sure to find you, John,
                To Nenagh fair.

The fair was just the same as then,
    Five years ago to-day,
When first you left the thimble men
    And came with me away;
For there again were thimble men
    And shooting galleries,
And card-trick men and Maggie men
    Of all sorts and degrees—
But not a sight of you, John-John,
                Was anywhere.

I turned my face to home again,
    And called myself a fool
To think you'd leave the thimble men
    And live again by rule,
And go to mass and keep the fast
    And till the little patch:
My wish to have you home was past
    Before I raised the latch
And pushed the door and saw you, John,
                Sitting down there.

How cool you came in here, begad,
    As if you owned the place!
But rest yourself there now, my lad,
    'Tis good to see your face;
My dream is out, and now by it
    I think I know my mind:
At six o'clock this house you'll quit,
    And leave no grief behind;—
But until six o'clock, John-John,
                My bit you'll share.

My neighbours' shame of me began
    When first I brought you in;
To wed and keep a tinker man
    They thought a kind of sin;
But now this three year since you're gone
    'Tis pity me they do,
And that I'd rather have John-John,
    Than that they'd pity you.
Pity for me and you, John-John,
                I could not bear.

Oh, you're my husband right enough,
    But what's the good of that?
You know you never were the stuff
    To be the cottage cat,
To watch the fire and hear me lock
    The door and put out Shep—
But there now, it is six o'clock
    And time for you to step.
God bless and keep you far, John-John!
                And that's my prayer.

Thomas MacDonagh

From Arigna they come—
Irish miles a full score—
From Croghan and Mohill,
From Ballinamore.

A gathering of side-cars,
Black in the street,
Slowly they move
Through the mist and the sleet.

Slowly they go
From the heel of the town,
Over the bridge
Through a bogland of brown.

Five score of cars,
Each with its load,
A dim, black file
On the white of the road.

Their talking is all
Of their cattle and care,
And him they will meet
No more at the fair.

His sayings and ways,
And the strength of his hand,
And the height of his deeds
In the war for the land.

And the evening is grey
Ere the tale is all told,
And the tired bones lie
In the quiet mould.

M.J. MacManus

In Sligo the country was soft; there were turkeys
    Gobbling under sycamore trees
And the shadows of clouds on the mountains moving
    Like browsing cattle at ease.

And little distant fields were sprigged with haycocks
    And splashed against a white
Roadside cottage a welter of nasturtium
    Deluging the sight,

And pullets pecking the flies from around the eyes of heifers
    Sitting in farmyard mud
Among hydrangeas and the falling ear-rings
    Of fuchsias red as blood.

But in Mayo the tumbledown walls went leap-frog
    Over the moors,
The sugar and salt in the pubs were damp in the casters
    And the water was brown as beer upon the shores

Of desolate loughs, and stumps of hoary bog-oak
    Stuck up here and there
And as the twilight filtered on the heather
    Water-music filled the air,

And when the night came down upon the bogland
    With all-enveloping wings
The coal-black turf-stacks rose against the darkness
    Like the tombs of nameless kings.

Louis MacNeice

83 GLASS FALLING

The glass is going down. The sun
Is going down. The forecasts say
It will be warm, with frequent showers.
We ramble down the showery hours
And amble up and down the day.
Mary will wear her black goloshes
And splash the puddles on the town;
And soon on fleets of macintoshes
The rain is coming down, the frown
Is coming down of heaven showing
A wet night coming, the glass is going
Down, the sun is going down.

Louis MacNeice

84 PROGNOSIS

Goodbye, Winter
The days are getting longer,
The tea-leaf in the teacup
Is herald of a stranger,

Will he bring me business
Or will he bring me gladness
Or will he come for cure
Of his own sickness?

With a pedlar's burden
Walking up the garden
Will he come to beg
Or will he come to bargain?

Will he come to pester,
To cringe or to bluster,
A promise in his palm
Or a gun in his holster?

Will his name be John
Or will his name be Jonah
Crying to repent
On the Island of Iona?

Will his name be Jason
Looking for a seaman
Or a mad crusader
Without rhyme or reason?

What will be his message —
War or work or marriage?
News as new as dawn
Or an old adage?

Will he give a champion
Answer to my question
Or will his words be dark
And his ways evasion?

Will his name be Love
And all his talk be crazy?
Or will his name be Death
And his message easy?

Louis MacNeice

85   A DYING ART

That day would skin a fairy—
A dying art, she said.
Not many left of the old trade.
Redundant and remote, they age
Gracefully in dark corners
With lamplighters, sailmakers
And native Manx speakers.

And the bone-handled knives with which
They earned their bread? My granny grinds
Her plug tobacco with one to this day.

Derek Mahon

86   ROISIN DUBH

(An earlier version of 'Dark Rosaleen')

Since last night's star, afar, afar,
    Heaven saw my speed;
I seemed to fly o'er mountains high
    On magic steed.
I dashed through Erne! The world may learn
    The cause from love:
For light or sun shone on me none,
    But Roisin Dubh!

O Roisin mine, droop not, nor pine;
    Look not so dull!
The Pope from Rome shall send thee home
    A pardon full;
The priests are near; O do not fear!
    From heaven above
They come to thee, they come to free
    My Roisin Dubh!

Thee have I loved, for thee have roved
    O'er land and sea;
My heart was sore, and ever more
    It beat for thee;
I could not weep, I could not sleep,
    I could not move!
For night or day, I dreamed alway
    Of Roisin Dubh!

The sea shall burn, the skies shall mourn,
    The skies rain blood,
The world shall rise in dread surprise
    And warful mood,
And hill and lake in Eire shake,
    And hawk turn dove,
Ere you shall pine, ere you decline,
    My Roisin Dubh!

James Clarence Mangan

I sell the best brandy and sherry,
To make my good customers merry;
    But at times their finances
    Run short, as it chances
And then I feel very sad, very!

Here's brandy! Come, fill up your tumbler;
Or ale, if your liking be humbler;
    And while you've a shilling,
    Keep filling and swilling—
A fig for the growls of the grumbler!

I like, when I'm quite at my leisure,
Mirth, music and all sorts of pleasure;
    When Margery's bringing
    The glass, I like singing
With bards — if they drink within measure.

Libation I pour on libation,
I sing the past fame of our nation
    For valour-won glory,
    For song and for story,
This, this is my grand recreation!

James Clarence Mangan

O Woman of Three Cows, *a gra!* don't let your tongue thus
    rattle!
Oh, don't be saucy, don't be stiff, because you may have
    cattle.
I have seen — and, here's my hand to you, I only say what's
    true —
A many a one with twice your stock not half so proud as you.

Oh, think of Donnell of the Ships, the Chief whom nothing
    daunted,
See how he fell in distant Spain, unchronicled, unchanted!
He sleeps, the great O'Sullivan, where thunder cannot rouse —
Then ask yourself, should *you* be proud, good Woman of
    Three Cows?

Your neighbour's poor; and you, it seems, are big with vain
    ideas,
Because, forsooth, you've got three cows — one more, I see,
    than *she* has;
That tongue of yours wags more at times than charity allows;
But if you're strong, be merciful — great Woman of Three
    Cows.

James Clarence Mangan

Errigal, like a high wave,
   Tossing a white crest,
Up from the sea of the moorland,
   Against the wind of the West.
Glorious the peak of Errigal:
   I love it all but best.

Muckish the swine-backed mountain,
   Seen in darkness dim,
Like the boar desired of Diarmuid,
   That, after wounding him,
Couches to rest in slumber,
   A bulk, gigantic, grim.

The Twelve Pins of Connemara,
   As sailing by I went,
Were a camp of Danaan heroes,
   For each of twelve a tent;
And the hosting of Lugh Lámh-fhada
   Was seen where the mists were rent.

The high reek of Holy Patrick,
   From over the island bay,
Is a cairn up-heaved by pilgrims
   Who hither came to pray;
But Slemish top is rounded
   As a farmer stacks his hay.

And it is not high Lurig Edain
   That looks from the Antrim shore,
Nor thy wooded slopes, Slieve Donard,
   Nor thy gates, O Barnes Mór.
Dear is each peak of Donegal,
   But there's one that I love more.

Look up from the streets of the city,
   Look high beyond tower and mast,
What hand of what Titan sculptor
   Smote the crags on the mountain vast?
Made when the world was fashioned,
   Meant with the world to last,
The glorious face of the sleeper
   That slumbers above Belfast.[1]

Alice Milligan

The historic Cavehill above Belfast has the profile of a human face.

90 SEA CHANGES

Each rock pool a garden
Of colour, bronze and
Blue gleam of Irish moss,
Rose of coral algae,
Ochre of sponge where
Whelk and starfish turn
In an odour of low tide;
Faint odour of stillness.

John Montague

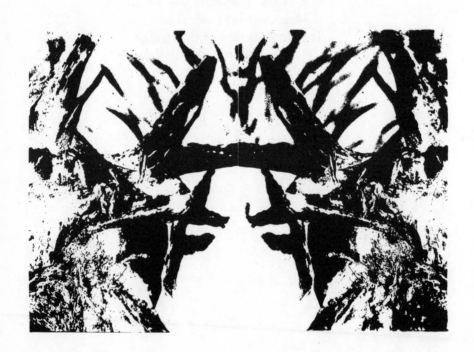

91 TIME OUT

The donkey sat down on the roadside
Suddenly, as though tired of carrying
His cross. There was a varnish
Of sweat on his coat, and a fly
On his left ear. The tinker
Beating him finally gave in,
Sat on the grass himself, prying
His coat for his pipe. The donkey
(not beautiful but more fragile
than any swan, with his small
front hooves folded under him)
Gathered enough courage to raise
That fearsome head, lipping a daisy,
As if to say — slowly, contentedly —
Yes, there is a virtue in movement,
But only going so far, so fast,
Sucking the sweet grass of stubbornness.

John Montague

What a view he has
of our town, riding
inland, the seagull!

Rows of shining roofs
and cars, the dome of
a church, or a bald-

headed farmer, and
a thousand gutters
flowing under the

black assembly
of chimneys! ...

He would be lost,
my seagull, to see
why the names on

one side of the street
(MacAteer, Carney)
are Irish and ours

and the names across
(Carnew, MacCrea)
are English and theirs

but he would understand
the charred, sad stump
of the factory chimney

which will never burn
his tail feathers as
he perches on it

and if a procession,
Orange or Hibernian,
came stepping through

he would hear the
same thin, scrannel
note, under the drums.

And when my mother
puts her nose out
once, up and down

the narrow street,
and retires inside,
like the lady in

the weather clock,
he might well see
her point. There are

few pickings here,
for a seagull, so
far inland. A last

salute on the flag
pole of the British
Legion Hut, and he

flaps away, the
small town sinking
into its caul

of wet, too well
hedged, hillocky
Tyrone grassland.

John Montague

93   A CANADIAN BOAT SONG

Faintly as tolls the evening chime
Our voices keep tune and our oars keep time
Soon as the woods on shore look dim,
We'll sing at St. Ann's our parting hymn.
Row, brothers, row, the stream runs fast,
The Rapids are near and the daylight's past.

Why should we yet our sail unfurl?
There is not a breath the blue wave to curl;
But, when the wind blows off the shore,
Oh! sweetly we'll rest our weary oar.
Blow, breezes, blow, the stream runs fast,
The Rapids are near and the daylight's past.

Utawas' tide! this trembling moon
Shall see us float over thy surges soon.
Saint of this green isle! hear our prayers,
Oh, grant us cool heavens and favouring airs.
Blow, breezes, blow, the stream runs fast,
The Rapids are near and the daylight's past.

Thomas Moore

Let Erin remember the days of old,
  Ere her faithless sons betray'd her;
When Malachi wore the collar of gold,
  Which he won from her proud invader,
When her kings, with standard of green unfurl'd,
  Led the Red Branch Knights to danger; —
Ere the emerald gem of the western world
  Was set in the crown of a stranger.

On Lough Neagh's bank, as the fisherman strays,
  When the clear cold eve's declining,
He sees the round towers of other days
  In the wave beneath him shining;
Thus shall memory often in dreams sublime,
  Catch a glimpse of the days that are over;
Thus, sighing, look through the waves of time
  For the long-faded glories they cover.

Thomas Moore

95 YEARS LATER

Whose is that hulk on the shingle
The boatwright's son repairs
Though she has not been fishing
For thirty-four years
Since she rode the disaster?
The oars were turned into rafters
For a roof stripped by a gale.
Moss has grown on her keel.

Where are the red-haired women
Chattering along the piers
Who gutted millions of mackerel
And baited the spillet hooks
With mussels and lug-worms?
All the hurtful hours
Thinking the boats were coming
They hold against those years.

Where are the barefoot children
With brown toes in the ashes
Who went to the well for water,
Picked winkles on the beach
And gathered sea-rods in winter?
The lime is green on the stone
Which they once kept white-washed.
In summer nettles return.

Where are the dances in houses
With porter and cakes in the room,
The reddled faces of fiddlers
Sawing out jigs and reels,
The flickering eyes of neighbours?
The thatch which was neatly bordered
By a fringe of sea-stones
Has now caved in.

Why does she stand at the curtains
Combing her seal-grey hair
And uttering bitter opinions
On land-work and sea-fear,
Drownings and famines?
When will her son say,
'Forget about the disaster,
We're mounting nets today!'

Richard Murphy

A shoulder of rock
Sticks high up out of the sea,
A fisherman's mark
For lobster and blue-shark.

Fissile and stark
The crust is flaking off,
Seal-rock, gull-rock,
Cove and cliff.

Dark mounds of mica schist,
A lake, mill and chapel,
Roofless, one gable smashed,
Lie ringed with rubble.

An older calm,
The kiss of rock and grass,
Pink thrift and white sea-campion,
Flowers in the dead place.

Day keeps lit a flare
Round the north pole all night.
Like brushing long wavy hair
Petrels quiver in flight.

Quietly as the rustle
Of an arm entering a sleeve,
They slip down to nest
Under altar-stone or grave.

Round the wrecked laura
Needles flicker
Tacking air, quicker and quicker
To rock, sea and star.

Richard Murphy

What shall we do for timber?
    The last of the woods is down.
Kilcash and the house of its glory
    And the bell of the house are gone,
The spot where that lady waited
    Who shamed all women for grace
When earls came sailing to greet her
    And Mass was said in the place.

My grief and my affliction
    Your gates are taken away,
Your avenue needs attention,
    Goats in the garden stray;
The courtyard's filled with water
    And the great earls where are they?
The earls, the lady, the people
    Beaten into the clay.

No sound of duck or geese there,
    Hawk's cry or eagle's call,
No humming of the bees there
    That brought honey and wax for all,
Nor even the song of the birds there
    When the sun goes down in the west,
No cuckoo on top of the boughs there,
    Singing the world to rest.

There's mist there tumbling from branches,
    Unstirred by night and by day,
And darkness falling from heaven,
    For our fortune has ebbed away,
There's no holly nor hazel nor ash there,
    The pasture's rock and stone,
The crown of the forest has withered,
    And the last of its game is gone.

I beseech of Mary and Jesus
   That the great come home again
With long dances danced in the garden,
   Fiddle music and mirth among men,
That Kilcash the home of our fathers
   Be lifted on high again,
And from that to the deluge of waters
   In bounty and peace remain.

Frank O'Connor

98   THE WATER-VOLE

He lives beneath the sally-hedge,
Beside the placid water's edge,
Within a bunch of foxes-sedge,
Growing on a moss-sprinkled ridge.

At close of day when he awakes,
He listens to the brown corncrakes,
The bullfrogs in the rushy brakes,
And dives and swims in nearby lakes.

D.J. O'Sullivan

Wild winter-rain comes plashing down
Turning the grey street jetty-brown;
Two cyclists skid, pedestrians rush,
Traffic policemen curse the slush.

On lamp-posts now few sparrows talk,
On roof-tops now less pigeons walk;
Only the Liffey sings a song
And gelid hail that hops along.

No shadow neath the Pillar lies,
Wind-drownéd are the newsboys' cries,
Gaunt and bare all the kerb trees stand,
Each tramway pole's a glinting wand.

D.J. O'Sullivan

Out on this rock in its mantle drab
    Thick mist comes stealing 'round the tower,
Ships' sirens moan and gulls' cries stab
    The air, as in the lee they cower;
Skies break: the sun's about to win
    Through cloud, and beam on every side;
Lag basking-shark show dorsal fin,
    Swim lazily against the west-going tide,
And fed, the otter comes to play
    Out on this rock. . . .

Out on this rock at sunset's glow,
    White spindrift on the lantern-pane
Sparkles and glistens, and runs below
    In rivulets of fire into the sea again.
A ghostly form comes floating down,
    Alights upon the flagpole's stay,
Great saucer eyes and speckled gown,
    An owl, bewildered by the ray;
And the lantern clock tocks time away
    Out on this rock. . . .

Out on this rock sweet moments come
    When memory glides on swiftest wings
To my childhood cot; a bent-thatched home;
    To an ivied church where a choir sings.
Then I kneel, and pray that when I grow old,
    When the Heavenly-Keeper my soul shall call,
He will knight me with a sword of gold,
    And end my lonesomeness 'midst loved ones all;
No lighthouse light, in The Light's 'fulgent ray
    Far from this rock. . . .

D.J. O'Sullivan

101 MOSAIC

Upon the waste-lands' tangled hem
The nettle glitters like a gem,
Variegated emerald, pink and white,
Each floral curve reflects the light.

A youthful Peacock butterfly,
Dancing in the sunny sky,
Alights to take a luscious sup
From the dangling nectar-cup.

As his probiscis sucks the mead
Of the tall leafy stinging weed,
His brown eye-marked wings outspread
O'er its fragrant flowering head.

Brown over green, pink under blue,
Shades and tints of auroral hue;
Butterfly and plant combine
To make an exquisite design.

D.J. O'Sullivan

On parachute threads,
Airborne,
At the winds' will.

Rising and falling,
Gossamer,
In radiant air.

Directional drift,
Skywards,
Seasonal movement.

Return to earth,
Settle,
Spider-silvered fields.

Dewdrops adorning,
Fabled,
Blessed Virgin's silk.

Alighting on Man,
Lucky:
Heralds of riches.

D.J. O'Sullivan

Chimney-perched
The Jackdaw
Calling 'Cae!'
Smoke enshrouded,
Black Beelzebub.

On a storm-tossed sea,
Rising and falling,
The Seagull
Better than any boat
Can take to the air,
Fly high.

Sky-hooked
Clothes-hanger,
The Windhover
Unslings,
Drops,
Death's arrow

Spring-usher,
Parasitic,
Onomatopoetic,
Mocking her victims,
Uneasy the nesting birds.

Barn-busker,
Up at dawn-light
Jangling his tune,
No care for tomorrow
Tattered his brown coat.

Crake
In the creaking corn
Shuttling.
Raucous
In search of love.

D.J. O'Sullivan

Here to the leisured side of life,
Remote from traffic, free from strife,
A cul-de-sac, a sanctuary
Where old quaint customs creep to die
And only ancient memories stir,
At evening comes the lamplighter;
With measured steps, without a sound,
He treads the unalterable round,
Soundlessly touching one by one
The waiting posts that stand to take
The faint blue bubbles in his wake;
And when the night begins to wane
He comes to take them back again,
Before the chilly dawn can blight
The delicate frail buds of light.

Seumas O'Sullivan

105   A PIPER

A Piper in the streets to-day
Set up, and tuned, and started to play,
And away, away, away on the tide
Of his music we started; on every side
Doors and windows were opened wide,
And men left down their work and came,
And women with petticoats coloured like flame
And little bare feet that were blue with cold,
Went dancing back to the age of gold,
And all the world went gay, went gay,
For half an hour in the street to-day.

Seumas O'Sullivan

106   THE SHEEP

Slowly they pass
In the grey of the evening
Over the wet road,
A flock of sheep.
Slowly they wend
In the grey of the gloaming
Over the wet road
That winds through the town.
Slowly they pass,
And gleaming whitely
Vanish away
In the grey of the evening.

Seumas O'Sullivan

107 TORTOISE

I had
a pet
tortoise
oh
a pet
tortoise
like
nobody else's
(nobody
else
I
knew
had
a pet
tortoise).
His head
was hard
as bark
his neck
(underneath)
soft as
a trick-
fountain-pen
snake's
his eyes
bird-bright.
I lacquered
his shell
to keep
it fresh.
He liked
fresh lettuce
ate it
voraciously

gallivanting round
the garden
more like
a hare than
a tortoise.
By night
I kept
him
in
a shed.
If I
forgot
maggots
crawled
next morning
inside
his shell
(I picked
them out
with a
match-stick).
In winter
he hiber-
nated
in a
box
in

our
coal-shed
beside a
black heap
of top
quality
English
coal.
That
was his
undoing.
One morning
in February
I found
him
quite
dead
under
two chunks
of it.
A pre-fab
tortoise-backed
tortoise-slack
tomb.
I buried him
cried
lied

to myself
No more pets.
Next year
I bought
a goldfish
the next
a budgie
the next
a hamster
— all three
are since
dead.

Pets
(any more
than people)
are not
for keeps.

Beekeepers
yes
gamekeepers
park-keepers even
are aptly
named
bird-fanciers
greyhound-breeders
horse-owners
cat-lovers
falconers even
— but who
ever heard
of a
tortoise-
keeper?

Basil Payne

Three boys
swinging
a dead cat
over a wall
do
you
find
that
funny?
I
don't
either
but
they didn't
look evil
to me
at all . . .

All
the same
they laughed
themselves silly
each time
the cat
didn't make it
over the wall
and cheered
when it did
at long last:
Heave-ho;
Heave-ho;
Hooray

One
Two
Three
And Away.
Maybe
(at that)
they weren't
guilty
maybe
the cat
simply died
of old age
distemper
pneumonia
heart-disease
maybe
the three
cat-swinging
cat-calling
boys
didn't
kill
it
at
all.

Anyway
they
got rid
of it
off the street
like good

upright
duty-doing
citizens
— no more
offence to
sore eyes
of passer-bys
(or spies).
Maybe
they laughed
simply
because
they
were just
as frightened
of death
as you
or I
(or even
the cat
was
before it
was dead).

What really
startles
is that
nothing
is as
dead as
a
dead
cat.

Basil Payne

My children
And I
Have a
Game
We play
Once or
Twice a
Month
When I
Am merry
i.e.
In need of
Distraction.
It's called
Realities.
Its simple
Really
Real
Simple.

I
Make faces.
They
Interpret.
I win
If they
Miss.
They never
Miss.
I lose
Always
Every time.

I scowl.
They clamour:
Angry?

Correct.

I sigh.
They cry out:
Worried?

Correct.

I grimace:
Disappointed?

Correct

I twine my fingers:
Frightened?

Quite correct.

Make sheeps' eyes:

Sorrowful?

Again correct.

I smile.
They yell out
(Cocksure)
Happy?

Correct.
(I say)
Correct.
Correct.
Now off to bed.
The game
Is over.

Over.
I know
When I'm beaten.

Basil Payne

The beauty of the world hath made me sad,
This beauty that will pass;
Sometimes my heart hath shaken with great joy
To see a leaping squirrel in a tree,
Or a red lady-bird upon a stalk,
Or little rabbits in a field at evening,
Lit by a slanting sun,
Or some green hill where shadows drifted by,
Some quiet hill where mountainy man hath sown
And soon will reap, near to the gate of Heaven;
Or children with bare feet upon the sands
Of some ebbed sea, or playing on the streets
Of little towns in Connacht,
Things young and happy.
And then my heart hath told me:
These will pass,
Will pass and change, will die and be no more,
Things bright and green, things young and happy;
And I have gone upon my way
Sorrowful.

Padraic Pearse

111   LULLABY OF A WOMAN OF THE MOUNTAINS

House, be still, and ye little grey mice,
Lie close tonight in your hidden lairs.

Moths on the window, fold your wings,
Little black chafers, silence your humming.

Plover and curlew, fly not over my house,
Do not speak, wild barnacle, passing over the mountain.

Things of the mountain that wake in the night-time,
Do not stir tonight till the daylight whitens!

Padraic Pearse

112   SEE THE CROCUS' GOLDEN CUP

See the crocus' golden cup
Like a warrior leaping up
At the summons of the spring,
'Guard turn out!' for welcoming
Of the new elected year.
The blackbird now with psalter clear
Sings the ritual of the day
And the lark with bugle gay
Blows reveillé to the morn,
Earth and heaven's latest born.

Joseph Mary Plunkett

142

I see his blood upon the rose
And in the stars the glory of his eyes,
His body gleams amid eternal snows,
His tears fall from the skies.

I see his face in every flower;
The thunder and the singing of the birds
Are but his voice — and carven by his power
Rocks are his written words.

All pathways by his feet are worn,
His strong heart stirs the ever-beating sea,
His crown of thorns is twined with every thorn,
His cross is every tree.

Joseph Mary Plunkett

Behold there came wise men from the east, saying, Where is he, for we have seen his star

It was a dark January night, cold and snowing
When the Three Kings started out
On their annual journey: and what on earth
They were doing — and such a time to be going!
And, honestly, what it was all about
Not one of them knew. But they wanted a birth,
A new lift, as we all do. Was the journey wise? —
Yes, or No? Well, that was anybody's guess
As it still is: a risk. A different address
May only land you in a different kind of a mess.
Put it no higher than that. But still, there was the Star
Throbbing in front like a bell, bobbing them on from afar,
Regardless of hail, rain, or snow, or glitter or glar.
The Three Kings marched away into the west,
To one dark enterprise they were addressed.

The Three Kings hitched their wagon to the Star
And gave the Star its head. Now near, now far,
Now in, now out, now to and fro it led;
Never straight. Journeys are always curly,
Like comets or like hairpins they are meant
To crown or to lead up to some event.
Herod did all he could do to prevent
Their coming. This journey had its hazards.
He broke the poles, and he cut the wires,
He stole their pump and deflated their tyres,
And he turned their messengers into liars;
But in vain.
He muffled the knocker, disconnected the bell,
Turned up his radio till it howled like hell,
Changed his name and address as well;
But in vain.

December now; the Three Kings stood
Benighted in the deepest wood,
The wits-end of their hardihood.
No longer kings, but helpless now
They threw away their golden bough;
They stamped upon their golden crowns
And damned the country, damned the towns.
They'd lost the Star, their only link
And anchor-light. O not a blink
No hope, no help in earth or sky!
— They gave a last despairing cry.
Then suddenly all raised a shout
For overhead the Star flared out
Just like a fan: and there they saw
In the last ditch, on the last straw,
In front of them a heavenly child.
See! it looked up at them and smiled.
It was the child within themselves
For which they'd sought, for which Age delves
— Now Age and Innocence can meet,
Now, now the circle is complete,
The journey's done. Lord, Lord, how sweet!

W.R. Rodgers

A mist opened and closed its eyes before him,
And in it he saw her looking at him
The untouchable terrible god.
O what ladders of longing led up from her
To him, what steps and depths of memory ran down;
He remembered the happy days in Galilee
When he was heaven's hub; the heap of smoking grass,
The bubble-pipe, the light upon the wall,
The children in the far garden looking for the lost ball,
And Mary calling him. He was always so distant
In those lonely days. O if only
He had mattered less, she wondered, if only
She had mastered him more, would he then
Have been like other men, a flat satisfied plain?
But no. In him mountains of onlyness rose
Snow-high. Dayspring was in his eyes
At midnight. And he would not come down
From his far purpose even for her who was
The root that raised him to this Cross and crown
Of thorns. Yet tenderly he spoke
Goodbye now, his voice choking and dry.
And as she went away, leaving him to die,
The vast moon of his cry rose up upon the darkness.
His heart broke.

W.R. Rodgers

116 ABOUT THE NINTH HOUR JESUS CRIED WITH A LOUD VOICE, SAYING, ELI, ELI, LAMA SABACTHANI?

His breath came in threads; his words were not his own.
He was dying now.
The sun refused to look, and the sky
closed up its eye. Only the windows of his wounds.
Were wide open, and the red curtains of blood
Blew out into the storm, torn to ribbons.
He could no longer fend death off.
Slow, slow, loath to go, hope holds up its head
Though feet are so sawn through, like a sawn tree that stands
Long, then with one blinding run and blundering tear
Of last despair, scattering its brains and branches on the air
Slumps, lumps, pitches headlong and thuds, a log clodded
      clean.
So his last cry and acquiescence. And the vast wall
Of people drew back before that dying fall.
God was dead.

W.R. Rodgers

(These last two poems are taken from a long work by
W.R.*Rodgers* called 'Resurrection: An Easter Sequence',
which deals with the crucifixion, death and resurrection
of Christ.)

In a quiet water'd land, a land of roses,
　　Stands Saint Kieran's city fair:
And the warriors of Erin in their famous generations
　　Slumber there.

There beneath the dewy hillside sleep the noblest
　　Of the clan of Conn,
Each below his stone with name in branching Ogham
　　And the sacred knot thereon.

There they laid to rest the seven Kings of Tara,
　　There the sons of Cairbré sleep —
Battle-banners of the Gael, that in Kieran's plain of crosses
　　Now their final hosting keep.

And in Clonmacnois they laid the men of Teffia,
　　And right many a lord of Breagh;
Deep the sod above Clan Creidé and Clan Conaill,
　　Kind in hall and fierce in fray.

Many and many a son of Conn, the Hundred-Fighter,
　　In the red earth lies at rest;
Many a blue eye of Clan Colman the turf covers,
　　Many a swan-white breast.

T.W. Rolleston

There are veils that lift, there are bars that fall,
   There are lights that beckon and winds that call —
      Goodbye!
   There are hurrying feet, and we dare not wait;
For the hour is on us, the hour of Fate,
   The circling hour of the Flaming Gate —
Goodbye, goodbye, goodbye!

Fair, fair they shine through the burning zone,
   Those rainbow gleams of a world unknown —
      Goodbye!
   And oh, to follow, to seek, to dare,
When step by step in the evening air
   Floats down to meet us the cloudy stair —
Goodbye, goodbye, goodbye!

The cloudy stair of the Brig o' Dread
   Is the dizzy path that our feet must tread —
      Goodbye!
   O all ye children of Night and Day
That gather and wonder and stand at gaze,
   And wheeling stars in your lonely way —
Goodbye, goodbye, goodbye!

The music calls and the gates unclose,
   Onward and upward the wild way goes —
      Goodbye!
   We die in the bliss of a great new birth,
O fading phantoms of a pain and mirth,
   O fading loves of the old green Earth,
Goodbye, goodbye, goodbye!

T. W. Rolleston

119 FROLIC

The children were shouting together
  And racing along the sands,
A glimmer of dancing shadows,
  A dovelike flutter of hands.

The stars were shouting in heaven,
  The sun was chasing the moon:
The game was the same as the children's,
  They danced to the self-same tune.

The whole of the world was merry,
  One joy from the vale to the height,
Where the blue woods of twilight encircled
  The lovely lawns of the light.

George Russell (AE)

Joe's no saint,
And I ought to know
For I work at the bench alongside Joe.
He loses his temper just like another
— Days he'd bite the nose off his mother,
And when I call for a pint of plain
Joe's not slow with 'The same again.'
He gives an odd bob to the poor and needy
But you wouldn't call him gospel-greedy
— You know what I mean? —
So if there's enquiries after he's dead
I won't swear to no haloes around his head,
For I never seen none.
When all's said and done
I don't suppose they give haloes out
To fellows who like their bottle of stout.

All the same, though,
I'm glad that I work alongside Joe.
For in the morning time I lie on
Long after Guinness's whistle is gone
And scarcely have time for a cup of tea
— As for prayers,
Well between you and me
The prayers I say is no great load —
A Hail Mary, maybe, on Conyngham Road
— You know how it is? —
The horn blows on the stroke of eight
And them that's not in time is late;
You mightn't get a bus for ages,
But if you clock late they dock your wages.

Joe, though,
He's never late at all,
Though he lives at the far end of Upper Whitehall:
And I happen to know
(For the wife's cousin lives in the very same row)
That he sets his alarm for half-past six,
Shaves, and goes through the whole bag of tricks
Just like a Sunday,
Gets seven Mass in Gaeltacht Park
And catches the half-seven bus in the dark.

In ways, too, he's not as well off as me,
For he can't go back home for a cup of tea —
Just slips a flask in his overcoat pocket
And swallows it down while he fills in his docket.
I do see him munching his bread and cheese
When I'm getting into my dungarees.

There isn't a thing about him then
To mark him off from the rest of men
— At least, there's nothing that I can see.
But there must be something that's hid from me —
For it's not every eight-o'clock-man can say
That he goes to the altar every day.

Maybe now you know
Why I'm glad I work alongside Joe.
For though I'm a Confraternity man
And struggle along the best I can
I haven't much time for chapel or praying,
And some of the prayers that Joe does be saying
Those dark mornings must come my way.
For if Joe there prays enough for three
Who has more right to a tilly than me?

When my time comes and they lay me out
I won't have much praying to boast about:
I don't do much harm, but I don't do much good,
And my beads have an easier time than they should.

So when Saint Peter rattles his keys
And says 'What's your record, if you please?'
I'll answer 'When I was down below
I worked at a bench alongside Joe.'

Joe is no saint with a haloed ring,
But I often think he's the next best thing,
And the bus that he catches at half-past seven
Is bound for O'Connell Bridge . . . and Heaven
— You know what I mean? —

John D. Sheridan

Ding dong didero,
   Blow big bellows,
Ding dong didero,
   Black coal yellows,
Ding dong didero,
   Blue steel mellows
Ding dong didero,
   Strike! — good fellows.

Up with the hammers,
   Down with the sledges,
Hark to the clamours,
   Pound now the edges,
Work it and watch it,
   Round, flat or square O,
Spade, hook, or hatchet —
   Sword for a hero.

Ding dong didero,
   Ding dong didero,
Spade for a labourer,
   Sword for a hero,
Hammer it, stout smith,
   Rightly, lightly,
Hammer it, hammer it,
   Hammer at it brightly.

George Sigerson

The long-rólling,
Steady-póuring,
Deep-trenchéd
Green billów:

The wide-topped,
Unbróken,
Green-glacid,
Slow-sliding,

Cold-flushing,
— On — on — on —
Chill-rushing,
Hush — hushing,

. . . Hush — hushing . . .

James Stephens

123 THE GOAT PATHS

(1)
The crooked paths
Go every way
Upon the hill
— They wind about
Through the heather,
In and out
Of a quiet
Sunniness.

And the goats,
Day after day,
Stray
In sunny
Quietness;
Cropping here,
And cropping there
— As they pause,
And turn,
And pass —
Now a bit
Of heather spray,
Now a mouthful
Of the grass.

(2)
In the deeper
Sunniness;
In the place
Where nothing stirs;
Quietly
In quietness;
In the quiet
Of the furze
They stand a while;
They dream;
They lie;
They stare
Upon the roving sky.

If you approach
They run away!
They will stare,
And stamp,
And bound,
With a sudden angry sound,
To the sunny
Quietude;
To crouch again,
Where nothing stirs,
In the quiet
Of the furze:
To crouch them down again,
And brood,
In the sunny
Solitude.

(3)
Were I but
As free
As they,
I would stray
Away
And brood;
I would beat
A hidden way,
Through the quiet
Heather spray,
To a sunny
Solitude.

And should you come
I'd run away!
I would make an angry sound,
I would stare,
And stamp,
And bound
To the deeper
Quietude;
To the place
Where nothing stirs
In the quiet
Of the furze.

James Stephens

The corn is down,
The stooks are gone,
The fields are brown,
And the early dawn
Grows slowly behind
Where the mountains frown,
And a thin white sun
Is shivering down.

There isn't a leaf,
Nor anything green,
To aid belief
That summer has been;
And the puffed-up red-breast
(Ball o' Grief)
Hops at the window
For relief.

The cows are in byre,
The sheep in fold;
The mare and the sire
Are safe from cold;
The hens are sheltered,
In wood and wire,
And the sheep-dog snoozes
Before the fire.

The farmer can grin,
As he rubs his hands,
For his crops are in
From the resting lands;
And his wheat is stored
In the oaken bin,
And his buxom wife
Makes merry within.

James Stephens

(1)
I cling and swing
On a branch, or sing
Through the cool clear hush of morning O!

Or fling my wing
On the air, and bring
To sleepier birds a warning O!

That the night's in flight!
And the sun's in sight!
And the dew is the grass adorning O!

And the green leaves swing
As I sing, sing, sing:
Up by the river,
Down the dell,
To the little wee nest,
Where the big tree fell,
So early in the morning O!

(2)
I flit and twit
In the sun for a bit,
When his light so bright is shining O!

Or sit, and fit
My plumes, or knit
Straw plaits for the nest's nice lining O!

And she, with glee,
Shows unto me,
Underneath her wing reclining O!

And I sing that Peg,
Has an egg, egg, egg!
Up by the oat-field,
Round the mill;
Past the meadow,
Down the hill;
So early in the morning O!

(3)
I stoop and swoop
On the air, or loop
Through the trees, and then go soaring O!

To group, with a troop,
On the skiey poop,
While the wind behind is roaring O!

I skim and swim
By a cloud's red rim;
And up to the azure flooring O!

And my wide wings drip,
As I slip, slip, slip,
Down through the rain-drops,
Back where Peg
Broods in the nest
On the little white egg,
So early in the morning O!

James Stephens

126 THE SNARE

I hear a sudden cry of pain!
There is a rabbit in a snare:
Now I hear the cry again,
But I cannot tell from where.

But I cannot tell from where
He is calling out for aid!
Crying on the frightened air,
Making everything afraid!

Making everything afraid!
Wrinkling up his little face!
As he cries again for aid;
— And I cannot find the place!

And I cannot find the place
Where his paw is in the snare!
Little One! Oh, Little One!
I am searching everywhere!

James Stephens

127 HERRINGS

Be not sparing,
Leave off swearing.
Buy my herring
Fresh from Malahide,
Better never was tried.
Come, eat them with pure fresh butter and mustard,
Their bellies are soft, and as white as a custard.
Come, sixpence a dozen, to get me some bread,
Or, like my own herrings, I soon shall be dead.

Jonathan Swift

128 A RIDDLE

We are little airy creatures,
All of different voice and features;
One of us in glass is set,
One of us you'll find in jet.
T'other you may see in tin,
And the fourth a box within.
If the fifth you should pursue,
It can never fly from you.

Jonathan Swift

Shaneen and Maurya Prendergast
Lived west in Carnareagh,
And they'd a cur-dog, cabbage plot,
A goat, and cock of hay.

He was five foot one or two,
Herself was four foot ten,
And he went travelling asking meal
Above through Caragh Glen.

She'd pick her bag of carrageen
Or perries through the surf,
Or loan an ass of Foxy Jim
To fetch her creel of turf.

Till on one windy Samhain night,
When there's stir among the dead,
He found her perished, stiff and stark,
Beside him in the bed.

And now when Shaneen travels far
From Droum to Ballyhyre
The women lay him sacks or straw,
Beside the seed of fire.

And when the grey cocks crow and flap,
And winds are in the sky,
'Oh, Maurya, Maurya, are you dead?'
You'll hear Patch-Shaneen cry.

John M. Synge

All in the April evening,
   April airs were abroad,
The sheep with their little lambs
   Passed me by on the road.

The sheep with their little lambs
   Passed me by on the road;
All in the April evening
   I thought on the Lamb of God.

The lambs were weary, and crying
   With a weak, human cry.
I thought on the Lamb of God
   Going meekly to die.

Up in the blue, blue mountains
   Dewy pastures are sweet;
Rest for the little bodies,
   Rest for the little feet,

But for the Lamb of God,
   Up on the hill-top green,
Only a cross of shame
   Two stark crosses between.

All in the April evening,
   April airs were abroad,
I saw the sheep with their lambs,
   And thought on the Lamb of God.

Katherine Tynan

Margaret Grady — I fear she will burn —
Charmed the butter off my churn;
'Tis I would know it the wide world over,
Yellow as saffron, scented with clover.

At Omagh market the witch displayed it:
Ill she had gathered, ill she had made it.
Hid in my cloak's hood, one glance I threw it,
Passed on smiling; my troth! I knew it!

Sheila, the kindest cow in the parish,
Mild and silken, and good to cherish,
Shame her own gold butter should leave her
To enrich the milk of a low-bred heifer!

I said not Yea or Nay to the mocker,
But called the fairy-man over from Augher;
Like a russet he is that's withered,
Bent in two with his wisdom gathered.

He touched the butter, he peered and pondered,
And crooned strange rhymes while I watched and wondered:
Then he drew me out through the gloaming
O'er the fields where the mist was coming.

He bewitched me so that I know not
Where they may grow, where they may grow not;
Those witch-hazels he plucked and plaited,
Crooning on while the twigs he mated.

There's the wreath on the churn-dash yonder.
All the neighbours view it with wonder;
And 'spite of Father Tom I avow it
The yield is doubled since that came to it

I bless the fairy-man though he be evil;
Yet fairy-spells come not from the Devil;
And Margaret Grady — I fear she will burn —
I do forgive her, with hate and scorn.

Katherine Tynan

Out upon the sand-dunes thrive the coarse long grasses,
    Herons standing knee-deep in the brackish pool,
Overhead the sunset fire and flame amasses,
    And the moon to eastward rises pale and cool:
Rose and green around her, silver-grey and pearly,
    Chequered with the black rooks flying home to bed;
For, to wake at daybreak, birds must couch them early,
    And the day's a long one since the dawn was red.

On the chilly lakelet, in that pleasant gloaming,
    See the sad swans sailing: they shall have no rest:
Never a voice to greet them save the bittern's booming
    Where the ghostly sallows sway against the West.
'Sister,' saith the grey swan, 'Sister, I am weary,'
    Turning to the white swan wet, despairing eyes;
'O,' she saith, 'my young one. O,' she saith, 'my dearie,'
    Casts her wings about him with a storm of cries.

Woe for Lir's sweet children, whom their vile stepmother
    Glamoured with her witch-spells for a thousand years;
Died their father raving, on his throne another,
    Blind before the end came from the burning tears.
Long the swans have wandered over lake and river.
    Gone is all the glory of the race of Lir,
Gone and long forgotten like a dream of fever;
    But the swans remember the sweet days that were.

Katherine Tynan

133 LES SILHOUETTES

The sea is flecked with bars of grey,
The dull dead wind is out of tune,
And like a withered leaf the moon
Is blown across the stormy bay.

Etched clear upon the pallid sand
The black boat lies: a sailor boy
Clambers aboard in careless joy
With laughing face and gleaming hand.

And overhead the curlews cry,
Where through the dusky upland grass
The young brown-throated reapers pass,
Like silhouettes against the sky.

Oscar Wilde

Under the rose-tree's dancing shade
   There stands a little ivory girl,
   Pulling the leaves of pink and pearl
With pale green nails of polished jade.

The red leaves fall upon the mould,
   The white leaves flutter, one by one,
   Down to a blue bowl where the sun,
Like a great dragon, writhes in gold.

The white leaves float upon the air,
   The red leaves flutter idly down,
   Some fall upon her yellow gown,
And some upon her raven hair.

She takes an amber lute and sings,
   And as she sings a silver crane
   Begins his scarlet neck to strain,
And flap his burnished metal wings.

With pale green nails of polished jade,
   Pulling the leaves of pink and pearl,
   There stands a little ivory girl
Under the rose-tree's dancing shade.

Oscar Wilde

135 THE FIDDLER OF DOONEY

When I play on my fiddle in Dooney,
Folk dance like a wave of the sea;
My cousin is priest in Kilvarnet,
My brother in Mocharabuiee.

I passed my brother and cousin:
They read in their books of prayer;
I read in my book of songs
I bought at the Sligo fair.

When we come at the end of time
To Peter sitting in state,
He will smile on the three old spirits,
But call me first through the gate;

For the good are always the merry,
Save by an evil chance,
And the merry love the fiddle,
And the merry love to dance:

And when the folk there spy me,
They will all come up to me,
With 'Here is the Fiddler of Dooney!'
And dance like a wave of the sea.

W.B. Yeats

The cat went here and there
And the moon spun round like a top,
And the nearest kin of the moon,
The creeping cat, looked up.
Black Minnaloushe stared at the moon,
For, wander and wail as he would,
The pure cold light in the sky
Troubled his animal blood.
Minnaloushe runs in the grass
Lifting his delicate feet.
Do you dance, Minnaloushe, do you dance?
When two close kindred meet,
What better than call a dance?
Maybe the moon may learn,
Tired of that courtly fashion,
A new dance turn.
Minnaloushe creeps through the grass
From moonlit place to place,
The sacred moon overhead
Has taken a new phase.
Does Minnaloushe know that his pupils
Will pass from change to change,
And that from round to crescent,
From crescent to round they range?
Minnaloushe creeps through the grass
Alone, important and wise,
And lifts to the changing moon
His changing eyes.

W.B. Yeats

137 TO A SQUIRREL AT KYLE-NA-NO

Come play with me;
Why should you run
Through the shaking tree
As though I'd a gun
To strike you dead?
When all I would do
Is to scratch your head
And let you go.

W.B. Yeats

138 THE SONG OF THE OLD MOTHER

I rise in the dawn, and I kneel and blow
Till the seed of the fire flicker and glow;
And then I must scrub and bake and sweep
Till stars are beginning to blink and peep;
And the young lie long and dream in their bed
Of the matching of ribbons for bosom and head,
And their day goes over in idleness,
And they sigh if the wind but lift a tress:
While I must work because I am old,
And the seed of the fire gets feeble and cold.

W.B. Yeats

I went out to the hazel wood,
Because a fire was in my head,
And cut and peeled a hazel wand,
And hooked a berry to a thread;
And when white moths were on the wing,
And moth-like stars were flickering out,
I dropped   the berry in a stream
And caught a little silver trout.

When I had laid it on the floor
I went to blow the fire aflame,
But something rustled on the floor,
And some one called me by my name:
It had become a glimmering girl
With apple blossom in her hair
Who called me by my name and ran
And faded through the brightening air.

Though I am old with wandering
Through hollow lands and hilly lands,
I will find out where she has gone,
And kiss her lips and take her hands;
And walk among long dappled grass,
And pluck till time and times are done
The silver apples of the moon,
The golden apples of the sun.

W. B. Yeats

NOTES and EXPLANATIONS

The first five poems in this collection have been so arranged to draw attention to the fact that they were all written originally in Irish in ancient times — between the 7th and 12th centuries. Later poems translated from the Irish have been placed under the names of the translators.

THE MYSTERY Said to have been written by Amergin, brother of Evir, Ir and Eremon, the first Milesian princes to land in Ireland, centuries before Christ. Probably one of the first poems written in Ireland.

THE HERMIT'S SONG The hermit is Marbhan, brother of King Guaire, who lived in the seventh century.

THE FAIRIES The fourth verse has not been included here.

MY SHIP Verses 2, 3 and 4 of the original have not been included here.

THREE COLTS EXERCISING . . . Tontine — the word comes from the name of an Italian banker, Tonti, who devised a life assurance scheme called a tontine. Here the name refers to a place of business.

I WISH AND I WISH This is the first verse only of a long poem.

BUTTERFLY IN THE FIELDS Etain, daughter of Etar, wife of Midir the Proud, a legendary princess who was changed into a butterfly by Midar's first wife. But she was reborn and married King Eocha. They had a daughter Etain Og.

THE LAST IRISH SNAKE
Aesculapius — a sacred snake worshipped in ancient Greece and Rome.
Batrachian — reptile; frog-like creature
blastoderm — the snake's eggs
Briarius — a legendary Greek monster with a hundred hands.
rodomontade — boasting; showing off

CHORUS OF SPIRITS Zephyr - the pagan god of the west wind, the west wind itself

LAMENT FOR . . . EOGHAN RUADH O'NEILL We have not included the refrain.

STILL LIFE WITH ASHTRAY & THE FLY IN THE TOWER Note that this poet uses a small 'i' instead of the usual capital 'I' when referring to himself. 'The Fly in the Tower' is a long poem, only the first verse being given here.

LAMENT FOR . . . THOMAS DAVIS Original verses 4-6 have been excluded.

THE CRAB TREE This is the first verse only of a much longer poem.

DOTAGE The title suggests somebody remembering the past with great affection

PATRICK MAGUIRE This is taken from a long poem 'The Great Hunger', the most famous of Patrick Kavanagh's poems.

CAOCH THE PIPER This is a shortened version of the original poem.

POEM FROM A THREE-YEAR OLD 'This poem is based on the bewildered outbursts and splutterings of a three-year-old child during a period of about two weeks when, for the first time, she became conscious of the fact of death. That consciousness soon passed, to be replaced by the habitual unawareness common to us all. During those two weeks, however, I wrote down some of the excited, rather frightened phrases uttered by the child. These phrases form the basis of this poem which subsequently I re-wrote many times.'
Brendan Kennelly.

COMBAT OF FERDIA AND CUCHULAINN These verses have been selected from different stages of the fight as recounted in the chapter 'Combat of Ferdia and Cúchulainn' in *The Táin*, translated by Thomas Kinsella.

Banba — Ireland

Scáthac, the Shadowy One, was a prophetess who taught both Ferdia and Cúchulainn the arts of war in Scotland (Alba)

AT CURRABWEE The Varder is a river in Greece, flowing into the Aegean sea.

BADGER This is the first section of the poem only.

ROISIN DUBH The fourth verse in the original has been excluded.

O'TUOMY'S DRINKING SONG — so called because the original version in Irish was composed by John O'Tuomy who lived from 1706-1775.

THE WOMAN OF THREE COWS There are six other verses in this great poem. The poem was originally composed in Irish sometime in the seventeenth century, but the author remains unknown.

MOUNTAIN SHAPES There are many other verses in this poem, which we have edited because of its length.

YEARS LATER This is the final section of a long poem called 'The Cleggan Disaster' which describes how five fishing boats were trapped off the west coast of Ireland in 1927 by a sudden storm, resulting in the drowning of sixteen fishermen from Rossadillisk and nine from Bofin.

WHAT A VIEW We have omitted ten verses from this poem because of its length.

KILCASH The original Irish version was written between the seventeenth and nineteenth centuries by an unknown poet.

SILHOUETTES The word 'onomatopoetic' here means that the name of the bird, the cuckoo, and the noise the bird makes, coo-coo, sound the same.

THE SHEEP This is the first verse of a long poem.

THE JOURNEY OF THE MAGI This is a shortened version of the original which is a very long poem.

THE DEAD AT CLONMACNOIS The original Irish version was composed by the poet Angus O'Gillan who lived in the fourteenth century.

SMITH'S SONG Originally written in Irish.

THE GOAT PATHS Section (4) of this poem has been omitted.

THE FIFTEEN ACRES The title of this poem comes from the name given to a portion of the Phoenix Park in Dublin.

THE POETS

William ALLINGHAM (1824-1889) Born in Donegal at Ballyshannon. Worked in local bank and later in the Customs service in London. Editor, playwright and poet, he is most famous for his graceful lyrical poems.
Christy BROWN Born in Dublin in 1932 almost completely paralysed. Learned to write and paint using his left foot — which gives the name to his famous autobiography, *My Left Foot.* **Died 1982.**
George BUCHANAN Born in Co. Antrim in 1904; went to Belfast University. He has written several novels *(Rose Forbes,* etc.) and plays, his best known being *War Song.* During the war he served in the RAF, and afterwards lived in Derry. He has published four volumes of poetry to date and now lives in London.
Joseph CAMPBELL (1879-1944) Born in Belfast, educated at St. Malachy's College. Lectured in the United States in the 1930s. Returned to live in Wicklow.
Austin CLARKE (1896-1974) Born in Dublin, educated at U.C.D. One of Ireland's great poets, he also wrote novels, verse drama and auto-biography.

Eilean Ni CHUILLEANAIN Born in 1942 in Cork city. Educated at
U.C.C. and Oxford. She now lectures in Trinity College, Dublin.

Padraic COLUM (1881-1972) Born in Longford. Has written novels,
biographies, plays and poetry. Spent much of his life in New York. A
great and popular poet.

George DARLEY (1795-1846) Born in Dublin and educated at T.C.D.
He spent most of his life in the London literary world.

Thomas DAVIS (1814-1845) Born in County Cork, educated at T.C.D.
With Gavan Duffy and Dillon he founded *The Nation*, and helped estab-
lish the Young Ireland movement.

Aubrey Thomas DE VERE (1814-1902) Born in Adare, Co. Limerick.
Became a Catholic in 1851. As well as the historical ballads for which he
he is best known, he wrote fine lyrics, and prose.

Denis DEVLIN (1908-1959) Born in Scotland of Irish parents. Educated
at U.C.D. and the Sorbonne. Worked for the Irish Foreign Service in
Washington, and later as Irish Ambassador to Italy.

H.L. DOAK (1890-1954) Born in Dublin, he had a distinguished career
at T.C.D. Headmaster of Cork Grammar School 1920-1922. As Editor
with the Talbot Press, he did much work in the educational field. *Three
Rock Road* and *Verdun and Other Poems* are two of his collections.

Desmond EGAN Born in Athlone. Has published two collections to
date, *Midland* and *Leaves.* He teaches in Newbridge College and has
edited textbooks for secondary schools.

Robert FARREN Born in Dublin in 1909, he taught for several years
and was a director of the Abbey Theatre. He wrote an extremely useful
book on Irish poetry called *The Course of Irish Verse*, and now works
with R.T.E.

Samuel FERGUSON (1810-1866) Born in Belfast and educated there
and in Dublin. A poet, lawyer and scholar, he is one of the most
important Irish writers of the nineteenth century.

Robin FLOWER (1881 - 1946) Born in England, educated at Oxford
and Dublin. Made an important contribution to studies of Irish life,
literature and history.

Oliver St. John GOGARTY (1878-1957) Born in Dublin. Worked as
a surgeon. Wrote books of literary reminiscences as well as poetry. A
senator from 1922-1936, and a witty conversationalist.

Oliver GOLDSMITH (1728-1774) Born in Co. Longford. Began to
study medicine but changed to literature. Famous for his plays and
his novel *The Vicar of Wakefield*. He died in London.

Eva GORE-BOOTH (1876-1926) Born in Sligo but spent most of her life in England. She was a sister of Countess Markeivicz.

Alfred P. GRAVES (1846-1931) Born in Dublin. Famous as a song writer, one of his best known songs is 'Father O'Flynn'. His son Robert is a well known poet.

Michael HARTNETT Born in 1941 in Kilmallock, Co. Limerick where he now lives. He has worked in England, and as a night-telephonist in Dublin. He has won several poetry awards and writes in English and Irish.

Seamus HEANEY Born in 1939 on a farm in County Derry. Educated at St. Columb's College and Queen's University, Belfast. He now lives in Wicklow. He has published four highly praised collections to date and is one of our finest poets.

John HEWITT Born in Belfast in 1907, he was educated at Queen's University. He has worked for the city museums in Belfast and in Coventry. He is one of the leading Ulster poets.

F.R. HIGGINS (1896-1941) Born in Mayo. Came to work in Dublin at the age of 14. He was editor of several journals, a Trade Union official, a friend of W.B. Yeats and Managing Director of the Abbey Theatre from 1935.

Nora HOPPER (Mrs Chesson) Born in Exeter in 1871. Her father was Irish and her mother Welsh. Most of her poetry reflects her deep attachment to Ireland (Date of death not ascertained).

Douglas HYDE (1860 - 1949) Born in Co. Roscommon. Founded the Gaelic League in 1893. He was professor of modern Irish at the National University. Became first President of Ireland. His numerous works and translations were the most influential force behind the Irish literary renaissance.

Valentin IREMONGER Born in Dublin in 1918. He has published several collections of poetry. A member of the Irish Foreign Service, he is currently Irish Ambassador to Luxembourg.

John IRVINE The poems here by Irvine come from 'A Treasury of Irish Saints' published posthumously in 1964 by the Dolmen Press. Irvine was an Ulster poet whose exquisite verse was very popular.

James JOYCE (1882-1941) Born in Dublin. Studied theology and medicine. Wrote a small amount of poetry, a collection of short stories, (*Dubliners*) and three great novels. He is one of Ireland's greatest artists, and his novels are masterpieces of English fiction.

Patrick KAVANAGH (1905-1967) Grew up on a small farm in Co. Monaghan. He was a very controversial figure among fellow writers in Dublin. Wrote some of Ireland's finest poetry, edited a newspaper, *Kavanagh's Weekly*, and wrote a famous novel, *Tarry Flynn*.

John B. KEANE Born in 1928 in Listowel where he now lives. Worked for some time in England. Ireland's most popular playwright, he also writes humerous essays and has published one volume of poetry.

John KEEGAN (1809-1949) Born in Laois, self-educated. Contributed poems to Davis' paper, *The Nation*. His work was very popular throughout the country.

Brendan KENNELLY Born in 1936 in Co. Kerry, educated at T.C.D. where he now teaches. He has published many volumes of poetry and two novels. He is a leading contemporary Irish poet

Thomas KINSELLA Born in 1928 in Dublin. Considered by many to be Ireland's leading poet today, he has published several volumes of poetry and a translation of *The Tain*. He lectures and teaches in Ireland and the United States.

Emily LAWLESS (1845-1913) Born in Kildare, she wrote historical essays, novels and poetry. She died in England.

Francis LEDWIDGE (1891-1917) Born in Slane. While working as a farm labourer he began to write poetry. He was killed fighting in France during the First World War.

Winifred M. LETTS Born in 1882, she has written several novels as well as poetry. She worked for the Abbey Theatre which produced two of her plays. (We have not ascertained the date of her death.)

Michael LONGLEY Born in Belfast in 1939. Educated in Belfast and Dublin. He works for the Arts Council of Northern Ireland, has published an anthology of verse for children and three volumes of poetry.

Donagh MACDONAGH (1912-1968) Born in Dublin, he was son of the poet and patriot, Thomas MacDonagh. He was best known as a verse dramatist.

Thomas MACDONAGH (1878-1916) Poet and patriot, Thomas MacDonagh was born in Tipperary. He studied for the priesthood but left to become a teacher and Irish scholar. He was executed for his part in the 1916 Rising.

Louis MCNEICE (1907-1963) Born in Belfast, educated at Oxford. A teacher and writer for the B.B.C. which he joined in 1941. He wrote radio plays and features as well as poetry.

Derek MAHON Born in Belfast in 1941 and educated at T.C.D. He spent some time in the United States and Canada and now lives in England.

James Clarence MANGAN (1803-1849) Born in Dublin. He had no formal education, was always poor and in ill-health. He had a flair for languages, particularly German. A bronze bust of Mangan stands in St. Stephen's Green, Dublin.

Alice MILLIGAN (1880-1953) Born in County Tyrone. With Eithne Carberry, another poetess, she founded and edited a nationalist literary paper called *The Shan Van Vocht*.

John MONTAGUE Born in Co. Tyrone in 1929, of a farming family. Educated at U.C.D. and York University. He is one of the leading poets of the younger generation. Teaches at U.C.C.

Thomas MOORE (1779-1952) Born in Dublin, the son of a grocer. He was educated at T.C.D. He became a popular figure in English society and famous for the lyrics he wrote for old Irish melodies. He died in England.

Richard MURPHY Born in Galway in 1927, he spent much of his early life in Ceylon. He was educated in England and now lives in Cleggan where he operates a sea-fishing boat to bring tourists to Inishbofin.

Frank O'CONNOR (1903 - 1966) Born in Cork, his real name was Michael O Donovan. He wrote novels, biographies, and powerful short stories for which he is world famous. He was a librarian, a Director of the Abbey Theatre and later a full-time writer. He spent some years in England and in the United States where he lectured at Harvard.

D.J. O'SULLIVAN Born in Co. Cork in 1906. Now retired, he worked as lighthouse keeper stationed off the Donegal coast. He is also well known as a naturalist.

Seumas O'SULLIVAN (1879-1958) Pen name of James Sullivan Starkey. He was for many years editor of an important literary magazine, *The Dublin Magazine*, and published several collections of poetry.

Basil PAYNE Born in Dublin in 1928. A critic and translator as well as a poet, he has lived in Germany and the United States.

Padraig PEARSE (1879-1916) Born in Dublin where he founded St. Enda's School. Wrote plays and poetry in English and Irish. Commander-in-Chief of the Irish Volunteers, he was executed for his part in the 1916 Rising.

Joseph Mary PLUNKETT (1887-1916) Born in Dublin, active in the Irish theatre and editor of the Irish Review. He was executed for his role in the 1916 Rising.

T. W. ROLLESTON (1857 - 1920) Born near Roscrea. He played an important role in the early literary revival. Scholar and translator, he worked in Germany and England in the latter part of his life.

George W. RUSSELL (1867 - 1935) Born in Co. Armagh. He used the pseudonym 'AE'. Poet, painter and mystic, he was a founder of the Irish Agricultural Cooperative Movement and gave great assistance to young writers.

W.R. ROGERS (1909-1969) Born in Belfast, he was a Presbyterian minister in Co. Armagh. He subsequently became a scriptwriter and producer for the B.B.C.

John D. SHERIDAN Born in 1903 in Dublin. Published novels and several collections of humourous essays. A teacher, he is one of the most popular of contemporary Irish writers. Died 1980.

George SIGERSON (1836-1925) Born in Strabane and educated in Cork and Paris. A scientist and writer, he won a distinguished reputation as a translator of Irish poetry.

James STEPHENS (1881-1950) Born in Dublin, he had no formal education. His writing attracted the attention of George Russell who encouraged him. His most famous book is the humorous story, *The Crock of Gold*, but his poetry is also very popular.

Jonathan SWIFT (1667-1745) Born in Dublin. The most famous satirist in the English language, author of *Gulliver's Travels*, he was Dean of St. Patrick's Cathedral in Dublin.

John Millington SYNGE (1871-1909) Born near Dublin and educated at Trinity College. A friend of W.B. Yeats, he was one of Ireland's greatest playwrights. His plays, *Riders to the Sea* and *The Playboy of the Western World* are known all over the world.

Katherine TYNAN (1861-1931) Born in Dublin and educated in Drogheda. She was involved in the Ladies Land League and wrote novels and poetry. Her married name was Hinkson. She died in London.

Oscar WILDE (1856-1900) Born in Dublin and educated at Trinity College and Oxford. His best known poem is *The Ballad of Reading Gaol*, but his reputation is based on his fiction and plays. His last years were spent in obscurity in France, where he died.

William Butler YEATS (1865-1939) Born near Dublin, his father was one of Ireland's leading painters. Yeats, the most influential poet of this century, also wrote plays and founded the Abbey Theatre in Dublin. He spent a lot of time in Co. Galway and became interested in Irish folk lore. He was made a Senator of the Irish Free State, and won the Nobel Prize for poetry. He died inFrance in 1939 and his body was brought back for burial at Drumcliff, near Sligo, in 1948.

Editors' note

In our selections we have aimed at providing the reader with a wide-ranging variety of styles and themes. We have not attempted to represent or do justice to poets; rather we have let the selections derive from a body of poems suitable for our purpose. Editors.

Acknowledgements

The publisher and editors offer their thanks to the many people who assisted, in various ways, towards the publication of this book: in particular, to Eilish Ryan; Dermot Larkin; Patrick Gillan; the librarians at Carysfort and St. Patrick's TTCs; the many poets who readily consented to the use of their poems; Gifford and Craven and Reprint Ltd. for efficiency and speed; and especially to Mr. John Gough NT, Conna, who first suggested the idea to the publisher.

The publisher and editors gratefully acknowledge permission to use copyright material.

For No. 11 from 'Come Softly to my Wake' to Mr. Christy Brown and Martin, Secker & Warburg Ltd. publishers. For No. 12 to Mr. George Buchanan; For Nos. 13 - 16 to Mr. Simon Campbell; For Nos. 17 - 18 To Mrs N. Clarke and The Dolmen Press; For Nos. 19 - 22 from *The Poet's Circuits* by Padraic Colum, published by Oxford University Press. Reprinted by permission of the Publishers; For No. 23 to Eilean Ni Chuilleanain and The Gallery Press; For No. 28 to The Dolmen Press; For No. 29 To Mrs Leslie V. Whitehead; For Nos. 30 - 31 to Mr Desmond Egan and The Goldsmith Press; For No. 32 to Mr Robert Farren; For No. 34 - 36 to Mr. O. Gogarty; For No. 40 - 41 to Mr. Michael Hartnett and The Gallery Press; For Nos. 42 - 46 from 'Death of a Naturalist' and Door into the Dark'. Reprinted by permission of Faber and Faber Ltd.; For No. 47 to Mr. John Hewitt; For Nos. 48 - 51 to Mrs. F. R. Higgins; For Nos. 53 to the author and The Dolmen Press; For Nos. 54 - 55 to The Dolmen Press; For Nos. 56 - 57 to the Society of Authors as the literary representative of the Estate of James Joyce; For Nos. 58 - 60 to Mrs Katherine K. Kavanagh; For No. 61 to Mr. J. B. Keane; For Nos. 4 - 5 and 63 - 68 to Mr Brendan Kennelly, and to Allen Figgis and Co. Ltd. Publishers, for Nos. 4 - 5, 63 and 65; For Nos. 68 - 71 to Mr Thomas Kinsella, and The Dolmen Press; For Nos. 82 - 84 from 'Collected Poems'. Reprinted by permission of Faber and Faber Ltd.; For No. 85 to Mr. Derek Mahon; For Nos. 90 - 92 to Mr. John Montague and The Dolmen Press; For Nos. 98 - 103 to Mr. D. J. O'Sullivan; and also to the Dundalgan Press (W. Tempest) Ltd. for Nos. 98 - 101; For Nos. 104 - 106 to Mrs E. F. Starkey's Estate; For Nos. 107 - 109 to Mr. Basil Payne and Gill and Macmillan publisher; For Nos. 114 - 116 from 'Europa and the Bull and Other Poems' by W. R. Rodgers to Martin, Secker & Warburg Ltd., Publishers; For No. 120 from a book of the same name. To Mr. John D. Sheridan. Rights of Reproduction in any form, and of public performance, strictly reserved by the author; For Nos. 122 - 126 from the Poems of James Stephens by permission of Mrs Iris Wise and Macmillan, London and Basingstoke; For Nos. 130 - 132 to the Society of Authors and Miss Pamela Hinkson; For Nos. 135 - 139 from the 'Collected Poems of W. B. Yeats' by permission of M. B. Yeats, Miss Anne Yeats and Macmillan of London and Basingstoke.
For nos. 95 & 96, from 'Sailing to an Island'. Reprinted by permission of Faber and Faber Ltd. For no. 78 to Mr Michael Longley;

In the case of a few poems we have been unable to make contact with copyright holders, and we would be grateful if they would contact the publishers.

FIRST LINE INDEX

A grey town in a country bare   36
A hiding turf, a green-barked yew-tree   3
A lone grey heron is flying, flying   50
A mist opened and closed its eyes before him   115
A Piper in the streets to-day   105
A shoulder of rock   96
A soft day, thank God!   76
After a few short hours its morning bowl   30
All day I hear the noise of waters   57
All I know is a door into the dark   45
All in the April evening   131
All year round the whin   46
Along the wandering strand the sea unloads glass balls   23
And will the flowers die   66
At a decent distance   67

Be not sparing   127
Beside yon straggling fence that skirts the way   37
Bespoke for weeks, he turned up some morning   44
Black tassels, black tassels, upon the green tree   19
By the still canal   65

Chimney perched   103
Colm had a cat   32
Cut from the green hedge a forked hazel stick   43
Come play with me   137

Dallán Dé! Dallán Dé! –   16
'Did they dare, did they dare, to slay Eoghan Ruadh O'Neill?'   25
Ding dong didero   121
Does any man dream that a Gael can fear?   26

Each rock pool a garden   90
Errigal, like a high wave   89
Every night at Currabwee   74

Faintly as tolls the evening chime   93
Far out to ocean Saint Patrick drove   18
For what this house affords us   48
Four ducks on a pond   10
From Arigna they come –   81

Gently! – gently! – down! – down!   24
Getting up early promises well   63
Golden stockings you had on   35
Goodbye, Winter   84

He lives beneath the sally-hedge 98
Here is the Crab-tree 34
Here's my story:the stag cries 4
Here to the leisured side of life 104
His breath came in threads; his words were not his own 116
His last days linger in that low attic 51
Hound of the bright deeds 69
House, be still, and ye little grey mice 111

I am Pangur Ban, my cat 2
I am patient, repetitive, multi-voiced 64
I am the wind which breathes upon the sea 1
I cling and swing 125
I do be thinking God must laugh 75
I dreamt last night of you John-John 80
I had a pet tortoise 107
I hear a sudden cry of pain! 126
I planted in February 60
I rise in the dawn, and I kneel and blow 138
I see his blood upon the rose 113
I sell the best brandy and sherry 87
I walked through Ballinderry in the springtime 33
I went out to the hazel wood 139
I wish and I wish 13
If I go by many a sloe bush 49
In a quiet water'd land, a land of roses 117
In Sligo the country was soft: there were turkeys 82
In your ghost, Dick King, in your phantom vowels I read 70
It was a dark January night, cold and snowing 114
It was all play, all sport 69
Joe's no saint 120

Kind Saint! Who loved the garden flowers 54

Lean out of the window 56
Let all the fish that swim the sea 39
Let Erin remember the days of old 94

Maeve held a ball on the dun 73
Margaret Brady — I fear she will burn — 130
My children and I 109

O to be blind! 15
O Woman of Three Cows, a gra! don't let your tongue thus rattle 88
O'er many a river bridged with ice 27
Oh I wish the sun were bright in the sky 21

Oh, to have a little house!   20
On a shrub in the heart of the garden   68
On parachute threads   102
On the edge of the springboard   28
One day he saw a daisy and he thought it   58
One shoulder up, the other down   29
One winter's day, long, long ago,   62
Only a fool would fail   5

Pushing the wedge of his body   78

See the crocus' golden cup   112
See, the pretty Planet!   8
Shaneen and Maurya Prendergast   129
Since last night's star, afar, afar   86
Slowly they pass   106
Somebody, when I was young, stole my toy horse   53
Spring, the Travelling Man has been here   77

10 by 12/ and a low roof   59
That day would skin a fairy   85
The animals are herded slowly from green fields   12
The beauty of the world hath made me sad   110
The cat went here and there   136
The children were shouting together   119
The corn is down   124
The crooked paths 123
The donkey sat down on the roadside   91
The fly in the tower   31 '
The glass is going down. The sun   83
The grand road from the mountain goes shining to the sea   38
The long-rolling / steady pouring   122
The mist hung on the slope, growing whiter   71
The night before Patricia's funeral in 1951   41
The night is on the dark sea wave   55
The pockets of our great coats full of barley   42
The sea is flecked with bars of grey   133
The sunflower bows upon her breast   52
There are veils that lift, there are bars that fall   118
There's famine in the land, its grip is tightening still   72
Three boys swinging a dead cat   108
Three colts exercising in a six acre   14
To Meath of the pastures   22
Today we carted home the last brown sheaf   47

Under the rose-tree's dancing shade   134
Up the airy mountain   9
Upon the waste-lands tangled hem   101

We are little airy creatures   128
What a view he has   92
What brings you here, Squinter   69
What little throat   6
What shall we do for timber   97
When God created water he must have thought of fish   79
When I play on my fiddle in Dooney   135
When I was a lad my bed was the ship   11
When moonlight   7
When night stirred the sea   17
Whom I ask for no gift   40
Whose is that hulk on the shingle   95
Wild winter-rain comes splashing down   99
With upturned bellies lying cold   61

ILLUSTRATION CREDITS

Terence O'Connell: drawings for poems 6, 16, 28, 39, 42, 45, 48, 52, 61, 68, 78, 92, 102, 103, 104, 131, 136

Dermot Larkin: photographs for illustrations for poems 3, 14, 50, 55 and 57, 90, 110,122.

Michael Cashman: photographs for illustrations for poems 7 and 8, 19, 43, 71, 91, 123.

TITLE INDEX *(References are to Poem Numbers)*

A Ballad of Athlone 26
A Canadian Boat Song 93
A Dream Dance 73
A Drover 22
A Dying Art 85
A Piper 105
A Poaching Song 79
A Rathlin Cradle Song 55
A Riddle 128
A Soft Day 76
About the Ninth Hour ... 116
Above 50
An Exile's Mother 72
At Currabwee 74
Autumn's End 61
Badger 78
Beech Tree 60
Black Tassells 19
Boy Bathing 28
Boys 75
Butterfly in the Fields 16
Caoch, the Piper 62
Chorus of Spirits 24
Combat of Ferdia and Cuchulainn 69
County Sligo 82
Dead Cat 108
Dick King 70
Dotage 49
Etched in Frost 124
Evidence 23
Four Ducks on a Pond 10
Frolic 119
Fun and Games 109
Galway 36
Getting Up Early 63

Girl in a Rope 65
Glass Falling 83
God's Praises 5
Goldenhair 56
Golden Stockings 35
Grace Before Beer 48
Herring is King 39
Herrings 127
High Island 96
I See His Blood Upon the Rose 113
I Wish and I Wish 13
Joe's No Saint 120
John-John 80
Kilcash 97
Lament for . . . Eoghan Ruadh O'Neill 25
Lament for . . . Thomas Davis 33
Leaf-eater 68
Les Silhouettes 133
Let Erin Remember 94
Lightening 67   Lightning 67
Load 47
Lullaby of a Woman of the Mountains 111
Money Spiders 102
Mosaic 101
Mountain Shapes 89
My Room 59
My Ship 11
My Story 4
Now there Stood by the Cross 115
O'Tuomy's Drinking Song 87
Pangur Ban 2
Patch Shaneen 129
Patrick Maguire 58
Poem from a Three Year Old 66
Prayer at Morning 40
Prognosis 84

Requiem for the Croppies   42
Roisin Dubh   86
Saint Fiacre   54
Sea   64
Sea Changes   90
See the Crocus' Golden Cup   112
Sheep and Lambs   130
Silhouettes   103
Smith's Song   121
Soliloquy of a Lighthouse Keeper   100
Spring, the Travelling Man   77
Still Life with Ashtray   30
Tara   71
Thatcher   44
The Animals   12
The Blackbird by Belfast Lough   6
The Blind Man at the Fair   15
The Bubble   8
The Cat and the Moon   136
The Children of Lir   132
The Country Funeral   81
The Crab Tree   34
The Dead at Clonmacnois   117
The Diviner   43
The Fairies   9
The Fairies in New Ross   7
The Fiddler of Dooney   135
The Fifteen Acres   125
The Fly in the Tower   31
The Forge   45
The Goat Paths   123
The Hermit's Song   3
The Journey of the Magi   114
The Lamplighter   104
The Last Irish Snake   18
The Little Waves of Breffny   38

The Main-Deep   122
The March to Kinsale   27
The Mystery   1
The Night before Patricia's Funeral   41
The Noise of Waters   57
The Old Jockey   51
The Old Woman of the Roads   20
The Painting   134
The Pets   32
The Planters Daughter   17
The Scarecrow   29
The Sheep   106
The Snare   126
The Song of Maelduin   118
The Song of the Old Mother   138
The Song of Wandering Aengus   139
The Sunflower   52
The Terrible Robber-Man   21
The Toy Horse   53
The Village Schoolmaster   37
The Water-Vole   98
The Wayfarer   110
The Witch   131
The Woman of Three Cows   88
Three Colts Exercising   14
Time Out   91
To a Squirrel at Kyle-na-no   137
Tortoise   107
What a View   92
Whinlands   46
Winter in Dublin   99
Years Later   95